LOST IN LEGEND

South Carolina's Coastal Ghosts and Lore

Bruce Orr

4880 Lower Valley Road • Atglen, PA 19310

Copyright © 2018 by Bruce Orr

Library of Congress Control Number: 2017955758

All rights reserved. No part of this work may be reproduced or used in any form or by any means—graphic, electronic, or mechanical, including photocopying or information storage and retrieval systems—without written permission from the publisher.

The scanning, uploading, and distribution of this book or any part thereof via the Internet or any other means without the permission of the publisher is illegal and punishable by law. Please purchase only authorized editions and do not participate in or encourage the electronic piracy of copyrighted materials.

"Schiffer," "Schiffer Publishing, Ltd.," and the pen and inkwell logo are registered trademarks of Schiffer Publishing, Ltd.

Designed by RoS
Cover design by Justin Watkinson
Type set in CloisterOpenFace BT/Chaparral Pro

ISBN: 978-0-7643-5545-5
Printed in the United States of America

Published by Schiffer Publishing, Ltd.
4880 Lower Valley Road
Atglen, PA 19310
Phone: (610) 593-1777; Fax: (610) 593-2002
E-mail: Info@schifferbooks.com
Web: www.schifferbooks.com

For our complete selection of fine books on this and related subjects, please visit our website at www.schifferbooks.com. You may also write for a free catalog.

Schiffer Publishing's titles are available at special discounts for bulk purchases for sales promotions or premiums. Special editions, including personalized covers, corporate imprints, and excerpts, can be created in large quantities for special needs. For more information, contact the publisher.

We are always looking for people to write books on new and related subjects. If you have an idea for a book, please contact us at proposals@schifferbooks.com.

"I get by with a little help from my friends . . ."

—The Beatles, 1967

I was a mean little kid. Well, not necessarily mean in the sense that I was wickedly evil. I was just wickedly mischievous. Growing up in Berkeley County, South Carolina, one of my favorite pastimes was collecting the spooky ghost tales of the area and scaring the ever-loving crap out of all the cute little girls in class. Most of the time I would change the story . . . writer's embellishment . . . to suit my needs, and I would often become the ill-fated lead character locked in a tomb, chased by sea monsters, or harassed by phantoms.

The author.... then. *Courtesy of Lost in Legend*

As fate would have it, those cute little girls grew up to be amazing women who now share the stories of the little snot-nosed brat who *never* grew up and became a much bigger kid who decided to go crawling around in tombs, chasing sea monsters, and harassing phantoms.

This book is dedicated to three of those little girls and the countless others who enjoy a good story, a great mystery, and a little adventure. It is also dedicated to my grandchildren, the next generation of explorers.

To my friends Renee, Karen, and Rhonda, this one is for you. It is also dedicated to all those who have shared in the adventures along the way.

To my grandchildren Lily, Noah, Annie, and Barrett (and all the future ones), this is for you. Put down the game controller, pick up a book, grab your bike, and go explore.

CONTENTS

Preface: *A Legal Basis for Ghosts—Developing Paranormal Probable Cause* 6
Introduction 12

Chapter 1: *Simply "Alice": Dancing on the Wrong Grave* 15
Chapter 2: *I've Never Heard of a Posquito* 23
Chapter 3: *Keeping My Promise to a Cross-Dressing Pirate* 29
Chapter 4: *Blackbeard's Blockade: The Day Venereal Disease Caused the Blockade of Charleston Harbor* 33
Chapter 5: *The Search for Poe's Gold* 39
Chapter 6: *The Curse of the Legare Tomb: Setting the Record Straight* 45
Chapter 7: *The Luck of the Irish: The Death of Daniel Hough* 51
Chapter 8: *I Don't Do Well with Witches: Hex Texting, Maleficium, and the Wreck of the* Margaret Scott 57
Chapter 9: *Root Magic: Paint, Police, and a Hoodoo Showdown* 67
Chapter 10: *Carolina Cryptids: South Carolina's Rampaging Reptiles* 75
Chapter 11: *A Paranormal Claims Study: Lunar Influence or Lunacy?* 81
Chapter 12: *Teeth, Trailers, Tropical Storms, and the Ghost of John Henry Rutledge (a.k.a. The Day I Learned I Could Cuss Underwater)* 85
Chapter 13: *The Lost Cannons of Battery Warren* 89
Chapter 14: *Lie or Legend? A Promise between Enemies* 95

Conclusion: *Final Thoughts* 107
Bibliography 108
Acknowledgments 110
About the Author 112

Preface

A LEGAL BASIS FOR GHOSTS: DEVELOPING PARANORMAL PROBABLE CAUSE

For something whose very existence has yet to be scientifically proven, ghosts sure have had an impact in the courts of the United States. In 1991, a New York court actually stepped in and ruled that a residence in Nyack, New York, was legally haunted, and in this particular action the ghosts existed as a fact of law. In *Stambovsky v. Ackley* 169A.D. 2d (NY App. Div. 1991), the New York Supreme Court Appellate Division ruled that a house which the owner had publicly claimed to be haunted was indeed legally haunted for the purpose of an action for rescission (overturning of the contract) brought forth by a subsequent purchaser of the house.

George and Helen Ackley and their family had frequently reported that their residence in Nyack, New York, was haunted. The 5,000 square foot Victorian home was subject to poltergeist activity. Items would mysteriously appear and disappear. Furniture would shake. Disembodied voices were heard and apparitions were seen. The family had publicly stated this, had reported it to the local newspaper on several occasions, and had an article published in *Reader's Digest* about the haunting.

The Ackleys eventually put the home up for sale and Jeffrey Stambovsky entered a contract to purchase the house. He made a down payment of $32,500 and agreed on a purchase price of $650,000. Neither the Ackleys nor their realtor disclosed to the purchaser any information about the haunting and the purchaser was unaware of the claims. When he later learned of the issues he filed an action requesting that the contract be broken due to fraudulent misrepresentation. A New York supreme court dismissed the case, but Stambovsky appealed.

The appellate court reversed the rescission issue and agreed that the claims of the house being haunted were something that the buyer could not easily research, and that the property was stigmatized by the claims. They allowed the contract to be broken.

In a majority ruling of three out of five justices the court stated that, " . . . having reported the ghosts' presence in both a national publication and the local press defendant is estopped to deny their existence and, as a matter of law, the house is haunted."

Stambovsky v. Ackley is not the first in which hauntings and ghosts became an issue. The testimony of a ghost actually helped convict a murderer in Greenbrier, West Virginia, in 1897.

So in civil law the existence of ghosts actually became legal fact, but what about criminal law?

In October 1896, Zona Heaster met a drifter by the name of Edward Stribbling Trout Shue who had come to Greenbrier County to work as a blacksmith. The two fell in love and married, despite the objections of Zona's mother, Mary Jane Heaster. She had a bad feeling about Shue.

Three months later, on January 23, 1897, Zona's body was discovered at her home by a young errand boy. Zona was found lying at the foot of her stairs. The boy ran home to tell his mother, who in turn contacted the local doctor, who was also the coroner. By the time the doctor arrived Shue had carried his wife back upstairs and placed her on the bed. He had redressed her in a high neck dress with a stiff collar and he had also placed a veil over her face. Shue cradled Zona's head, sobbing.

The coroner noted that this was unusual due to the tradition of women of the community washing and dressing a deceased female. He also shortened his examination of the corpse due to the husband's apparent grief; Shue reacted so violently to the examination that the doctor left the residence.

Zona's cause of death was listed as "Everlasting faint," but was later changed to "childbirth" due to the fact that she had been treated by the doctor for female issues a few weeks earlier.

Zona was buried the next day. During the wake a grieving Shue would allow no one to come close to the coffin, and he remained at the head of the coffin the entire time. He also placed a pillow beside Zona's head on one side and a rolled up sheet on the other side, stating that he hoped this would help her to rest easier. After the wake Zona's mother had an opportunity to remove the sheet prior to her child's burial. She offered the sheet to Shue, who refused it. Zona's mother took the sheet home with her after the burial.

When Zona's mother returned home she noticed that the sheet had an odd smell. She subsequently washed the sheet, and when she dropped the sheet into the water the water turned red. Soon the sheet turned pink and the water cleared. The stain could not be removed from the sheet, and the grieving mother took this as a sign that her child had been murdered.

For four weeks Mary Jane Heaster prayed that she would learn what had happened to her child. Exactly four weeks after the funeral Zona visited her mother. Initially Mrs. Heaster thought this was a dream. Zona informed her mother that Shue was abusive and had murdered her. He had killed her because he believed that she had not adequately prepared his dinner. He had snapped her neck, and to prove it the ghost turned her head around until it was facing backward. The ghost continued to visit her mother for the next three consecutive nights as an apparition.

Zona's mother was convinced that her daughter had been murdered. She visited the local prosecutor, John Alfred Preston, and told him of the ghostly visits. Apparently she sparked enough interest that the prosecutor sent out investigators to question several witnesses, including the coroner, Dr. Knapp. After the initial interview Preston went and questioned Dr. Knapp himself. Dr. Knapp admitted that he had not been able to make a complete examination of the body. This was sufficient cause to exhume the body and conduct an autopsy.

On February 22, 1897, Zona's body was exhumed. The protests of her husband were ignored and he was required by law to be present at the autopsy. Zona's neck was broken, her windpipe smashed, and there were finger mark bruisings around her throat. Also interesting was that the ligaments in her neck were torn and ruptured, and the neck was dislocated between the first and second vertebrae, which would allow the head to rotate around backward. Shue was immediately arrested.

Shue was placed in jail, and while he was awaiting trial it was learned that Zona was actually his third wife. His first wife had divorced him due to abuse. The second wife had mysteriously died less than a year after they had wed. While in jail Shue admitted to reporters that he had indeed been married three times, but his intended goal was to have seven wives.

The trial began on June 22, 1897, and the prosecutor did all that he could to avoid the issue of Zona's ghostly visits. Interestingly enough, Shue's attorney did not. He brought up the issue of the ghost in an effort to discredit the witness, but his plan backfired, and Zona's testimony was allowed. Zona actually testified in her own trial by proxy through her mother.

Since the defense had actually introduced the matter, the judge had no obligation to instruct the jury to ignore the ghostly hearsay. Shue was subsequently convicted of murder and sentenced to life in prison. He died in West Virginia State Penitentiary just three years into his sentence.

Cases such as these have always intrigued me. Having been a criminal investigator, I have always been fascinated by how evidence is used and introduced to prove or disprove guilt or innocence. In both of these cases the existence of ghosts became a fact of law and their existence was not disputed. So does this mean that the evidence points to the fact that ghosts do exist? Are ghosts real? A few years ago I set out to try and answer this question for myself.

At first I was not sure if I believed in them or not. When asked about ghosts, I often responded that I believed in the possibility of ghosts, yet I had never had that one "beyond a shadow of a doubt" experience. I had many interesting occurrences, but not anything that I was willing to go out on the proverbial limb for and defy all scientific reasoning and logic. One day, as I poked and prodded along on my quest, I ran into an older lady who basically told me that if I kept poking my nose around in the places that I poked my nose around in and questioning things best left alone, I had better be prepared for the answers because sooner or later I would get more than I bargained for. That is pretty much paraphrasing her statement, but I got the gist and prodded on. I never paid much attention to that statement because I thought I was prepared. I was not.

The funny thing about ghosts is the more that you look into them and the more that you uncover about them the more questions you have. Then you push harder, things get weirder, and you begin to question if what actually just happened actually just happened. Still, you keep poking. You get sucked into a world that you cannot prove to others, because the more you try to prove it to yourself, the more you deny what you are actually witnessing. Why?

Because when we were young we accepted things. As we grew older we were taught to challenge what we had readily accepted. Things that were acceptable fell into a category that we called normal. Then there were those things that fell outside the range of normal, and we were told that these things did not exist. Therefore, all things paranormal—or outside the norm—are not real.

But what happens when the paranormal and the normal merge?

When we were young, we would wake up every Christmas morning to a paranormal event. Toys and presents would be mysteriously left in our homes for good little boys and girls. We would be told that a big fat man in a bright red suit had left them for us. We readily accepted that at face value as it was told to us, and we believed in it. We were given an explanation to something that was beyond the normal and it was accepted.

If you really think about that, it is kind of creepy. What do you think would have happened if our parents told us that a big fat stranger was going to fly through the sky, slither down our chimney, sneak in our house with a bunch of tiny elves, and watch us while we slept? You never know if those elves could have crawled under our beds as we were sleeping while the old fat guy watched us while we slept and he checked his naughty list in the dark, trying to figure out what to do about naughty kids. Obviously presentation goes a long way.

As we grew older, eventually we discovered a scientific and acceptable explanation for the paranormal event that brought the new toys. Our minds as children held on to the belief that Santa did exist long enough for us to grow older and wiser, and investigate the matter in an effort to prove that there was a more logical explanation.

And as we grew older we outgrew certain ideas. We investigated and explained the things that we could and we dismissed the things that we could not adequately explain. Things like ghosts.

But what if "ghost" is just another name for something that is scientifically explainable? What if we are outright dismissing something that truly does exist and can eventually be scientifically explained? What if we drop the word and all the negative and unscientific ideation that the word presents and focus on finding an explanation to what many folks are actually experiencing?

Maybe if we took the approach that something may indeed exist, and then tried to figure out what that actually may be, then we may get somewhere. In other words, resurrect that acceptance that you had as a child and then combine it with the wisdom and knowledge that you have as an adult and do not just shrug it off. That is the approach I was forced to take when logic and reason flew out the window.

It sure made things easier a bit farther down the road.

I loved ghost tales growing up. I loved the spooky and scary and the dead that did not stay dead. In that world ghosts existed. Then I grew up and became a homicide investigator. I saw the dead and I worked around them. Dead is dead and you do not come back. Wow, what a vast difference.

After retiring, I wanted to start looking into the tales that I enjoyed as a kid, but I chose to do it with the knowledge of an investigator. As a kid I believed in ghosts, but as an adult I was much more skeptical. Somewhere along the way I experienced a few things that made me open to the possibility that there was something there. As a kid it was easy to accept and move on. As a detective, I was used to finding answers and I wanted answers. Answers were found in research and investigation. I was used to the results of an investigation leading to answers. I wanted answers.

Well, the old woman was right. I got more than I bargained for, and I was not prepared for the answers I got.

Almost immediately when I began researching ghost tales I became involved with a house that had an unusual reputation. This was an older residence in which many folks encountered the ghost of a praying soldier. What made this a little more twisted is the fact that this soldier appeared to be wearing a blue uniform. This would make him a praying Union soldier in the middle of the South. Based on my training I went into full investigator mode.

After an extensive amount of historic research I discovered that a Confederate field hospital had once stood on the grounds where this house was built. That literally brought the Civil War to their doorstep, but that does not explain why a Union soldier was praying there. Further research discovered that after the war and during reconstruction, the Union occupied the hospital. In fact, I identified the commanding officer as Col. James Beecher; he commanded the 35th US Colored Troops and was also a reverend. Historic research is now tying this story together, much to my amazement. I was asking all the right questions and getting all the right answers. I was not prepared for the answers I was getting, but I moved forward.

Now what do you do as a criminal investigator when you develop the identity of a suspect and you have a witness? You prepare a photo lineup. I did just as I would any other case and presented six photos to a woman who had seen the praying soldier, except that this lineup consisted of bearded Civil War soldiers that had been dead for over a century.

She picked him out. I was not prepared for that. I honestly expected failure and that would be the end of it. I was one hundred percent sure that there was no way in hell anyone would identify Beecher. Now I had discovered historic evidence to back up a ghostly claim, plus eyewitness identification of my suspect from a photo lineup. In the real world that is called probable cause, and I would go get a warrant. What do you do when you have real-time probable cause that would stand up in the real world identifying something that is scientifically unproven to exist, unreal, and therefore does not exist in the real world?

Probable cause exists when apparent facts are discovered through logical research and investigative methods that would lead a reasonably intelligent and prudent person to believe that a criminal event did occur. It is a reasonable belief based on facts that can be articulated.

I had just developed probable cause that a man who died in 1886 was praying over my witness 125 years later. I was also positive that my witness had no knowledge who my suspect was or how I had developed him.

This forced me to rethink my approach. It took a bit, but I had to accept the fact that my investigation proved that there was probable cause to believe that the improbable existed and that this ghost was real.

So what about all the others? . . . And that is how it started.

Col. James Beecher

INTRODUCTION

So what is a "Ghostorian?" On my tax returns I am listed as a historian, so as far as the federal government is concerned I am a historian. Oddly enough, the truth of the matter is the history I research is usually associated with a ghost tale, folktale, or some other legend. Thus, the name "ghost historian" or "ghostorian" was created to describe the research I do. It was a name given to me by Kevin Kane—a producer with the reality show *Ghost Hunters*—during correspondence on a few episodes they were developing in the Charleston area. I told him I was going to use it. He said go ahead, and feel free to put it on business cards. I did and have been using it ever since.

So how does one become a ghostorian? I was your typical brat of the '70s. There was no internet, video games, cellular phones, or computers. You went outside and explored. I also grew up on local legends and ghost tales as a kid. One of my favorite books was *Charleston Ghosts* by Margaret Rhett Martin. Within that book is a story called "The Wayfarer at Six Mile House." This is a tale about a couple, John and Lavinia Fisher, who ran an inn on the outskirts of Charleston in the 1800s. The lovely couple would take in boarders, prepare them a hot meal, and then, unbeknownst to the guest, sedate them with hot tea laced with oleander. Then, according to the tale, they would murder their sleeping guests. There was a trapdoor under the bed, and the recently deceased would be robbed and disposed of through that trapdoor . . . *under the bed*.

It was that " . . . under the bed . . . " part of Ms. Martin's tale that often bothered me as a child and gave me the nightmares that prompted my father to tell my mother to take "that damned book" away from me. Tales of homicidal maniacs, dead bodies, and decaying skeletons under the bed did not mix well with my young imagination, but as fate would have it, that changed when I reached adulthood. In a strange twist of irony, I would become a homicide investigator and spend a lot of time around homicidal maniacs, dead bodies, and decaying skeletons.

In 2010, I revisited this tale of Lavinia Fisher. Having recently retired from law enforcement, I opted for this story because it concerned the alleged first female serial killer executed in America. After researching the story as an adult and seasoned investigator, it did not take long to learn that the facts of John and Lavinia Fisher got overshadowed by the fiction and lost in legend. The result was *Six Miles to*

Charleston—the True Story of John and Lavinia Fisher, which took an in-depth look at the legend and turned it upside down with historic fact.

A year later I found myself telling ghost tales around a campfire, and I was surprised that none of the young folks I was telling these tales to actually knew any of them. These were the same kids that earlier that day swam with manatees and watched American bald eagles soaring across our camp. We had talked about how sad it was that these creatures were endangered and that future generations may never see them.

After telling these tales to this younger generation, I also realized that these legends may one day disappear and no one will hear them. It was in that moment I decided I would make an effort to research and preserve legends and folklore for the future and Lost in Legend was born. I never knew that six years later this "hobby" would become a business that included historical research that would be archived by the state, maritime research and dive projects with archaeologists, consulting for numerous paranormal television programs, interviews, and lectures. It would also allow me the opportunity to meet many wonderful people interested in the same goal I was: to explore the unexplained, track down a pirate, look for buried treasure, or chase a ghost. It would also allow me to write several books on the research, including this one, although this one is a little different than its predecessors.

This is not your typical "ghost" book. In fact, a number of the tales involve legends and folklore outside the paranormal. For the past decade I have been exploring the state of South Carolina, researching legends, folklore, and ghost tales, and compiling that research with the intent of presenting those tales with the history behind them. This book incorporates a portion of those projects. In the following stories you will read about historical figures, Native Americans, African Americans, pirates, and phantoms that have created the folklore and legends I grew up with. What makes this book different is unlike so many others, you will also get an account of the history behind those legends, a few anecdotes, and several personal experiences, as I researched and investigated each tale with my friends and colleagues. It is my hope that the reader will find this combination unique and entertaining. It is also my hope that you enjoy these tales as much as I did exploring the history behind the hauntings and the facts behind the folklore.

The grave of Alice Belin Flagg. *Courtesy of Lost in Legendv*

1

SIMPLY "ALICE"
Dancing on the Wrong Grave

At All Saints Church on Pawleys Island, South Carolina, there are many graves within the gates of the manicured graveyard. They are adorned with headstones of different shapes and sizes—some traditional and others much more elaborate. They mark the lives of all those who rest there. Many have elegant wording, and others have scriptural references. All of them are marked with two dates: a birth date and a date of death. These dates are separated by a dash or hyphen signifying the entire life of the person that lies beneath each stone.

Within the gates of this graveyard there lies another grave in stark contrast to the others. The area around this grave is barren, for no grass will grow there. Upon this grave lies a large stone. Upon this stone there are no elegant phrases. There are no dates and no hyphen to mark the life of the girl the stone commemorates. Upon this stone is engraved but a single word, "ALICE."

In contrast to her gravestone, the life of Alice Belin Flagg was far from simple. She was born on November 29, 1833, into a very prominent family of physicians that had settled in Murrells Inlet, South Carolina. Her grandfather, Dr. Henry Collins Flagg, served under Gen. Washington as surgeon general in the Continental Army. He served alongside the likes of Gen. Lafayette and Gen. Casimir Pulaski. Pulaski, originally from Poland, was a hero throughout Europe, and had impressed Benjamin Franklin to the point that he recommended him to Washington to become a member of the cavalry within the Continental Army. It was Dr. Henry Collins Flagg that actually removed Pulaski's leg after the battle of Savannah in an attempt to save the general's life.

Alice's father Eben Flagg was also a physician. Alice was one of seven children born to Dr. Eben Flagg and his wife Margaret Belin, who was also from a prominent family. Two of her siblings died in 1822: one was three years old and the other was two. Two other siblings died in infancy. Alice and her two older brothers, Arthur and Allard, were the only three children that survived. Like their father, Arthur and Allard became physicians. Had times been different Alice may have become one too, but at this point in American history that was not the case. She was expected to become a socialite in keeping with the family status.

In 1838, when Alice was only five years old, her father died. Her brother Allard became the head of the household at age eighteen and was expected to help his widowed mother raise his two younger siblings and guide them into living up to their elite social status. All three children carried their mother's maiden name and their father's last name, and Dr. Allard Belin Flagg was determined that Arthur Belin Flagg and Alice Belin Flagg exceeded those expectations.

Allard had little issue with his younger brother. Arthur lived up to his expectations, kept to his studies, and followed in the family tradition by also becoming a physician. Young headstrong Alice was a much different story. Arthur was also not much help to Alice, and in an effort to avoid his brother's wrath often sided with Allard regarding family matters and their troublesome sister.

It was touch and go for the next ten years; Allard was able to keep Alice on track, but his attention was now divided. He was busy running a successful medical practice and had begun construction on the Hermitage, a new home in Murrells Inlet. His attention to fifteen-year-old Alice began to slip as he focused on other things.

One day Alice informed him that she had a young suitor. Allard could tell that she was very much infatuated with the man. As Allard questioned her he was able to determine that the young man was in the turpentining business. Turpentining was a growing industry, and along with rice production had made many landowners throughout the South very wealthy. The pines of the plantations were tapped and their resin was harvested. The resin was then introduced to a distilling process and turpentine was produced. The product not only had uses as fuel and a solvent, but was also used in the medical field as a treatment for everything from abrasions and chest rubs to the treatment of head lice. Alice was excited, and was sure that this information would please her domineering brother. Her brother was indeed intrigued by the prospect and an arrangement was made for the young man to come and call upon young Alice.

The day came to pass, and the young suitor arrived in a buggy drawn by a team of fine bay horses. The young man introduced himself, then asked to take Miss Alice for a ride. He was informed by Allard that he had saddled his own horse for the young man to ride and that Allard would accompany his young sister in the buggy; the suitor could ride beside it and converse with Alice. The fact that the impetuous young man had expected Alice to leave her home on a buggy ride unchaperoned angered Allard. This placed doubts in the doctor's mind about the young man's character and had him questioning his upbringing. By the end of this ride his suspicions were confirmed.

During the ride Dr. Allard Flagg learned all he needed to know about the young man. He was not from a wealthy or prominent family. He was not a landowner, nor even a professional man. The young man that his sister had become so enamored with was nothing more than a salesman in the turpentine industry. A lowly salesman! Allard was infuriated, and immediately upon returning to the Hermitage he forbade his sister from ever seeing the man again. The more Alice pleaded the more infuriated Allard became. Allard's heart was hardened and Alice's heart was broken.

In complete defiance of her brother Alice professed her love for the man and told him that she intended to marry him. The fact that Alice was determined to trade her family name for the name of a nobody who would likely be forgotten to history sent Allard into a rage the likes of which Alice had never witnessed before. Within the next few days Dr. Allard Flagg had made arrangements for his sister to be shipped off to a boarding school in Charleston—perhaps time away from the Inlet would help her forget the young man. He also hoped the four-day journey to the "Holy City" would dissuade the young man from following Alice in attempts to pursue the relationship, but Allard was wrong. The young suitor did indeed follow Alice to Charleston and they continued to pursue their relationship in secret.

On New Year's Eve 1849, Alice attended the Saint Cecilia Society Ball in Charleston. The society, named after the patron saint of music, was formed in 1766 as a concert society, and its annual concert series was the most sophisticated in North America for over fifty-four years. By 1820, the concerts were replaced by an annual ball, and it was at this ball that all the young and refined debutante southern ladies were introduced to society. It was on this night that Alice Belin Flagg was presented to the world. It was also the night that Alice was presented with an engagement ring. Once her young suitor placed it on her finger she swore she would never take it off again. This was the happiest night of the young girl's life, and even the pesky mosquitoes of Charleston could not annoy her.

Not many days after the ball Alice began to feel ill, but aches, fever, chills, and vomiting could not dampen her spirits. Fortunately the flu-like symptoms lasted only a few days and Alice bounced back. She seemed to do well for about a week, but then her symptoms returned with a vengeance.

As Alice became more ill her abdominal pain became severe. When her skin started becoming yellow and she began bleeding from her nose the school sent for her brother. Even in her weakened state Alice knew that her brother would become furious at the news of her engagement, so she placed the ring on a ribbon and tied the ribbon around her neck, hiding it under her gown.

Dr. Allard Belin Flagg and his servants set out on the four-day journey and retrieved Alice. Not only had Alice's skin turned yellow by this time, but so had the whites of her eyes. Allard realized that his sister was dying from Yellow Fever, a disease he had seen take the lives of countless people. Most of the wealthy fled the areas toward the mountains of the upper state to avoid the disease, and in fact their mother had done just that. In 1838, a Yellow Fever epidemic decimated the population of Charleston, and the wealthy learned to flee for self-preservation. The cycle seemed to be repeating itself ten years later, and in fact in another ten-year cycle a similar epidemic would once again sweep through Charleston. The 1858 epidemic would be so brutal that in one church alone (St. Matthew's German Evangelical Lutheran Church) the congregation would be cut in half by 308 deaths.

By the time Allard arrived in Charleston, Alice's liver and kidneys were beginning to fail. She was slipping in and out of consciousness, and the few fleeting moments that she was conscious were shrouded in a state of confusion and delirium. Allard knew that there was little he could do for her other than take her back home to the Hermitage to live out her final days.

The four-day trip back to Murrells Inlet was hard on Alice. The servants carried her into her room in the yet-unfinished home and began to tend to her needs. Allard also began to treat his sister. It did not take him long to decipher the dying girl's ramblings and he soon discovered the ring. As the young girl lay unconscious he snatched the ring from around her neck. In a rage he stormed out of the Hermitage, ran down to the water's edge, and with all his might flung the ring out over the inlet, and into the murky waters it fell.

It was not long after that Alice began crying out for her ring. Servants would hear crashing sounds and enter the room to find the girl had fallen out of bed in a complete state of delirium and was attempting to crawl around the floor, searching for the ring. The servants would place her back in the bed and for a while would appease her by searching for the ring themselves. It was at this point that Allard decided to give her a substitute, and he placed another ring on her finger in an effort to trick the girl and calm her fits. Alice removed the ring and threw it across the room. "I want my ring!" she screamed. "Keep your ring Allard, I shall find my own." These were the last words Alice ever spoke to her brother. Just twenty-four days after the happiest night of her life Alice Belin Flagg died. She was only fifteen.

Because of the fear of the disease spreading Alice was quickly buried across the roadway at Cedar Hill Church. Her mother had not even had time to return from upstate. Her body was buried on January 25, 1849. On February 2, a service was held at All Saints Church and a marker was placed at the sight. The marker simply stated, "Alice."

Even in death Alice was not safe from her domineering brother. Since Alice was ready to surrender her family name in exchange for a nobody's name he deprived her of the privilege of having it engraved on her stone. Perhaps the next Alice would live up to the name bestowed upon her. You see, Allard's new wife was pregnant, and on October 21 of the following year she gave birth to a baby girl that Allard promptly named Alice Belin Flagg.

Not long after Alice died the servants began claiming that they had seen her at the Hermitage searching for her ring. Many of the servants began to leave trinkets as offerings on her gravestone at All Saints Church in an effort to appease her. Allard dismissed the ghostly claims as foolish and went on about his life, as did his brother, Arthur.

Dr. Arthur Flagg did little to help his sister in life, and perhaps it was this guilt that led him to follow in Allard's footsteps, but in 1889, he too had a child which he immediately named Alice Flagg. Perhaps this was too much for the restless spirit. She had been deprived of her happiness in life by one brother as the other turned a blind eye and a deaf ear to the cruelty. Now both had replaced her by naming their daughters after her.

Nature has an interesting way of repaying injustice, and on Friday, October 13, 1893, it did just that. The very waters that Dr. Allard Belin Flagg cast his sister's ring into in a fit of anger rose up in a rage of its own and came crashing down on Murrells Inlet. In the aftermath of the storm the shorelines were strewn with bodies. Upwards of 2,000 people perished in what would be now classified as a category 3 hurricane that struck the coast a few miles northeast of Georgetown.

The storm surge hit Magnolia Beach, now known as Huntington Beach. Many of the Flagg family resided there, including Dr. Arthur Flagg and his family. Two of Arthur's sons had also built residences there, and Dr. Allard Flagg's son, also named Allard, also resided there. By the time the storm ended Dr. Allard Belin Flagg stood in the yard of the Hermitage, looking out across the marsh, and realized, much to his horror, that not a single house remained. Allard's son—called Cousin Allard to distinguish between the two—survived the storm. He and a manservant had realized they had missed their opportunity to escape. As the waters rose the two waded across to the barn and released his horse in hopes that it would have a fighting chance at survival. The two then fought their way back across the waist-deep water and climbed the stairs into the elevated home. It was not long before the waters reached the door and began covering the pine floorboards of the home. The two climbed up to the second floor, but soon the waves crushed the house and the roof collapsed on top of them, forcing them to escape through the back windows.

As the men were being swept away they began to cling to debris as it passed by them. Soon what appeared to be a large raft drifted by and they grabbed on to it. They soon realized it was actually the roof of the home's separate kitchen building. As they climbed on to the makeshift raft they realized it already contained one additional passenger, the house cat.

As the men and the cat were being swept inland they soon became aware of a large, dark object moving in the water toward their direction. Cousin Allard soon realized it was his own horse which he had released only moments earlier. As he spoke to the horse, the horse swam alongside the raft as best he could. Soon the raft crashed against the trees and the men grabbed on to them with all their might. The horse, unable to reach bottom, continued on toward shore.

When the storm was over Cousin Allard, his servant, and the cat were all found alive, clinging to the tree. Legend has it that their fingers had to be forcefully pried away from the branches. Cousin Allard's horse also survived the storm and was later discovered wandering about the destruction.

Dr. Allard Flagg's brother Arthur was not as fortunate. Arthur, his wife Mattie, and their children, Albert, Ward, Ebin, Mattie, and Alice, were all killed. The storm would soon be known as the Flagg Flood for the large numbers of Flagg members it killed. Dr. Arthur Belin Flagg and his family are memorialized at All Saints Church. Their bodies were never located. Dr. Allard Belin Flagg survived the storm to live with this knowledge until his death in 1901.

Alice's grave is still marked with trinkets left behind by visitors. Legend has it that persons that walk around her grave thirteen times backwards are able to speak to her. Others say that any young girl who runs around the grave nine times with her eyes closed will open them to find her ring missing. Not far from Alice's stone there is another that stands tall. It is mere feet from Alice's and stands in stark contrast to the young girl's barren grave. It is that of her brother, Dr. Allard Belin Flagg. As in life so as in death, Allard still stands domineering over his little sister.

I first heard of Alice's story as a young boy. My mother had relatives in Murrells Inlet and often visited them. While there she became acquainted with the owner of the Hermitage, Clarke A. Willcox. The house was completed by Dr. Allard Belin Flagg in 1849. After his death in 1901, the house went to his daughter, Alice. She did not keep it long. Perhaps it was the continued sightings of her namesake that prompted her to sell in 1904 to Mr. S. S. Fraser, who in turn did not stay long and sold it the following year to Edgar Beaty in 1905. Beaty kept the house for five years, then sold it to Mr. Willcox's father in 1910. This family did not seem troubled by the ghost and accepted her existence.

I began researching the tale as an adult through *Lost in Legend*. First of all, many folks insisted that Alice Belin Flagg never truly existed and was a character Mr. Willcox created in an effort to sell his books and attract guests to tour the Hermitage. Obviously that was quickly dispelled by research at All Saints Church and Belin United Methodist Church. (Belin United Methodist Church was built on Cedar Hill, the place where—according to records—Alice is physically buried.)

Most of the story that I have presented to you was taken from narratives from Mariah Heywood, who was a servant to the Flagg family. Ms. Heywood was about eight years old when Alice died and was witness to the events. She passed the story down to Mr. Willcox and his niece, Genevieve Peterkin. Other information was gathered through archival research, as well as with the assistance of local historian Katherine Durning.

Interestingly enough, some additional notes of interest to this tale arose during research.

Charles Fraser was an American painter famous for his miniature portraits. Fraser was born in Charleston, South Carolina, and established his career as an artist there. In winter 1857, a collection of his work was brought together for an exhibition in Charleston. The printed catalog for the exhibition contains 313 miniatures. One of his works is of a dark-haired young teenage girl and the portrait is entitled "Alice Belin Flagg." It is believed to be the only existing record of what Alice looked like, and is believed to have been made sometime during the year prior to her death. That would indeed have placed her in Charleston to sit for the portrait, and this would also coincide with her being enrolled in school in Charleston in 1849.

Also of note is that during this time a very prestigious school for girls existed at 39 Legare Street in Charleston. It was operated by Madame Talvande. Madame Talvande was no stranger to young girls and scandal. In 1828, fifteen-year-old Maria Whaley attended the school. Her father was Col. Joseph Whaley of Pine Barron Plantation on Edisto Island. In an interesting twist of irony, he too had chosen to send his young daughter to boarding school in an effort to end her relationship with an undesirable man named George Morris. It did not work, and one night the young lady slipped away and eloped with Morris at St. Michael's Church before returning to the school. The next day, much to Madame Talvande's horror and great scandal, George Morris retrieved his bride.

 Painting of Alice Belin Flagg by Charles Fraser

Madame Talvande immediately erected a high wall around the school. The wooden gates remained until 1838, when the city placed an order for cast iron work to be done for a newly built guardhouse. The gates were created, but were deemed too elaborate and costly for the city, and were then secured by Madame Talvande for the entrance of the school. The newly installed gates did deter further elopements, but it also gave a name to the incident that necessitated their installation. (The incident with Mr. and Mrs. Morris is known in Charleston history as the "Sword Gates Romance.")

The fact of this incident and Madame Talvande's efforts to deter future elopements would have made this an ideal location for Allard to place Alice.

The school closed in 1849. Perhaps the school closed on its own, or perhaps the fact that Alice's relationship continued and she was engaged while under the school's care had an impact after the infamous "Sword Gate Romance." This would have made Alice a member of the final class at Madame Talvande's School for Girls.

While researching the history of Gen. Casimir Pulaski I located an interesting tale. The fact that Dr. Henry Collins Flagg removed Pulaski's leg is documented on a petition by the doctor's wife to receive his Revolutionary War pension after his death.

While history states that Pulaski was mortally wounded in 1779, at the Siege of Savannah, there is a discrepancy as to what happened to his body. One account holds that he died and was buried a few miles south of Savannah at Greenwich Plantation. Another account states that after Pulaski was wounded he was taken aboard the privateer merchant brigantine ship the *Wasp* under the command of Capt. Samuel Bulfinch. When gangrene set in the wound, his leg was amputated in an effort to save his life, but he subsequently died. Charles Litomisky, a fellow soldier from Pulaski's Polish homeland, claims he helped bury his body under a large tree on the bank of a creek approximately fifty miles from Savannah traveling toward Charleston. In 1962, work crews on Fripp Island working near Old House Creek uncovered skeletal remains that were determined to be over one hundred years old. Most interesting is the fact that the skeleton was missing a leg.

The Hermitage has long since been removed, relocated, remodeled, and renovated, and there seems to be no new reports of Alice's appearances there. All Saints Church is another story. There are many who perform the rituals and claim to have experiences with Alice's ghost despite the fact that she is not there and that they are quite literally dancing on the wrong grave.

Pottery sherds. *Courtesy of Lost in Legend*

2

I'VE NEVER HEARD OF A POSQUITO

While in Murrells Inlet researching the Alice Belin Flagg legend, I met with a wonderful historian named Katherine Durning. She was an expert on the legends and folklore of Murrells Inlet and the surrounding areas. Even though elderly, she began to chauffeur me around the area and show me all the historic sites at Wachesaw Plantation, including the footings and foundation of a home that once belonged to Rev. Allard Belin.

Belin had purchased the property around 1800, before moving over to Murrells Inlet and building a church. Documents show that the reverend sought permission from the Methodist church to erect a church, parsonage, kitchen, stables, and other buildings on a property known as Cedar Hill. This is the very property on which Alice Belin Flagg is actually buried, and what would later become the location of Belin United Methodist Church.

Ms. Durning also showed me the foundations of houses belonging to the founding fathers of Murrells Inlet, including that of Capt. John Murrell. These were in close proximity to a bluff overlooking the Waccamaw River known as Mills Bluff. This is when the conversation turned to the Native Americans that once inhabited the area.

As we stood on the bluff discussing "Indians," I informed Ms. Durning that I was a diver and had a working relationship with the state's Maritime Research Division (MRD)—a division of the South Carolina Institute for Archaeology and Anthropology (SCIAA)—and that I had recently been involved in a project with archaeologist Dr. Chester DePratter in search of Yemassee Indian pottery in the ACE Basin, consisting of the Ashepoo, Combahee, and Edisto Rivers.

I explained to her that the Combahee is considered a blackwater zero visibility dive, and that it was quite difficult to locate pottery twenty feet down on the bottom of a river when you could not see. I also told her that the visibility was so bad on that project that what I had thought was my dive partner bumping into me on the bottom actually turned out to be a medium-sized alligator who had mistaken me for a possible lover.

May is alligator mating season, and part of the mating ritual is for the male gator to blow bubbles under the female's chin. This young gator had obviously realized that there were bubbles coming from this long, dark figure lying on the bottom and she had come in to investigate. After nudging me a few times, she obviously realized I was not her type once she saw the lights, and instead of devouring me she moved on in search of love elsewhere. All this for a few fragments—ah, the things I do for history.

Ms. Durning laughed at the story, and advised me that there was a far easier method to recovering pottery fragments, or sherds. She then proceeded to tell me the story of what she called a Posquito. I had never heard of a Posquito, so I was intrigued.

Ms. Durning explained that as a child she had been told that Mill's Bluff had once been a location where Native Americans gathered annually for a ceremony of renewal called the Posquito. The legend had been handed down verbally in the area for generations, and in fact several burial mounds were located on the property when it was being cleared for a golf course. She stated that all the area's tribes would meet at this location and destroy all their old wares, settle all disputes, and extinguish all village fires. They would then ignite one new fire, and the elders of each tribe would carry embers back to their respective villages and ignite their own fires.

According to the legend, this was done yearly to close out the old year and bring in the new year clean and fresh. She said this continued for eons until an epidemic wiped out the area tribal communities. She then said, "I want to show you something." At this point Ms. Durning led me down the bluff to the shoreline. "Look," she said as she pointed toward the sandy shoreline, and for as far as I could see the area was littered with pottery fragments. The fragments were eroding out of the bank, washing out into the river, and then being redistributed along the shoreline.

I began gathering pottery sherds and placing them in a plastic bag that Ms. Durning furnished. After gathering about two pounds worth I felt I had retrieved enough. I immediately made a phone call to the Maritime Research Division and spoke with archaeologist Nate Fulmer. Nate and I had attended the same field training course sponsored by the division and had become friends. I became a volunteer research diver. He later became employed by them, and he and his supervisor, Ashley Deming, had become a great resource and a wealth of information when I had run across anything strange in the field.

The author surveying and graphing an artifact scatter with the South Carolina Maritime Research Division. *Courtesy of Lost in Legend*

When I returned home, I made an appointment to meet up with Nate and Ashley with the pottery fragments. In the interim I had begun identification of the fragments, but being out of my element, I wanted to have the two archaeologists examine the sherds. After reviewing the items it was determined that—including the plastic SOLO cup I had collected off the shore—I had recovered items as recent as the night before to as far back as 2500 BC.

In the collection there were many distinct and varying patterns of Native American pottery covering all ages. There were also fragments of pottery known as Colonoware, which was manufactured by slaves. There were items identified as salt-glazed fragments, Westerwald, Whiteware, and Pearlware from the colonists and others that had inhabited the area.

Completed identification of pottery fragments.
Courtesy of Lost in Legend

But what did this mean and what about the Posquito?

Having now identified the collected fragments, I set about to determine if this mysterious ceremony had indeed existed. I soon learned that the Southeastern Native American culture had a ceremony that the new European settlers had named the "Busk." It was also called the "Green Corn Ceremony," and was performed by most tribes as a cleansing and purification of the social order.

Further research disclosed that the tribes themselves had several different names for it, but the Creek Indians called theirs the "Poskita," which literally means "to fast." Fasting was a large part of the purification process and ritual, so the name had slightly changed through oral tradition and translation, but what Ms. Durning had described to me was indeed accurate.

The Green Corn Ceremony was significant to all of the Southeastern tribes; the Creek, Chickasaw, and Cherokee were just a few that participated. The term "People of One Fire" is still used today, and is in fact a nationally recognized alliance of the Southeastern tribes. The fact that the fragments were eroding from and washing out of the embankment lends more credibility to Ms. Durning's legend, and that the site was indeed used for this ceremony. As a historian, I love when I stumble headfirst into a legend and the facts seem to support the tale, and the conglomeration of pottery sherds seem to do just that. It also told another tale that is much more tragic.

Eons of Native American fragments were at the scene. Fragments from two periods—the Woodlands and the Mississippian—were intermixed with that of a few centuries of colonization by the settlers. When the European settlers first arrived, they brought many new things to the Native American population. They began giving them names such as Creek, Cherokee, and Chickasaw. They also gave them diseases the likes of which Native Americans had never experienced.

Native Americans had never been exposed to the diseases prevalent on the distant continent and had not developed natural immunities, nor developed the medicinal means to combat them. Illnesses such as smallpox, measles, chickenpox, and typhoid soon decimated populations. On average it is estimated that between twenty-five to fifty percent of most tribes were wiped out. Other tribes were completely decimated.

It was the eons of Indian fragments, a few centuries of colonial fragments, the legend, and the name of the location that told a tale that had been repeated throughout Native American populations over and over again. During the Green Corn Ceremony villages would conduct trade among themselves. The area soon became a hub for the tribes to conduct trade and became a center of commerce. After the introduction of settlers trade continued between the Native Americans and the colonists, and disease was introduced. Soon the area's Native American population was decimated.

It is said that after the epidemic destroyed the villages the laughter and happiness of the ceremony disappeared and was soon replaced by the wailing of mothers crying for their daughters and fathers crying for their sons. The remaining survivors named the area "Wachesaw," meaning "Place of Great Weeping."

It is said that the earth never forgets, and that the area was washed in the tears of the grieving. It is also said that quite often on quiet nights in the early Fall, when the corn is green, you can still hear the sounds and disembodied voices of the first inhabitants of the area validating its name.

The Old Exchange Building

3

KEEPING MY PROMISE TO A CROSS-DRESSING PIRATE

A few years ago I was asked to do a book signing at the Old Exchange Building and Provost Dungeon in Charleston. The building was constructed circa 1761, and was originally the location where visiting dignitaries and royal governors arrived and were greeted. The building would later play a prominent role in the creation of South Carolina's government and the development of the United States.

On December 3, 1773, citizens of Charleston—then Charlestown—met there to protest the British Tea Tax. That meeting is considered the first of the South Carolina General Assembly and the birth of the state of South Carolina's present government. The taxed tea was seized and stored there until it was sold to finance the growing patriot cause. The building would also soon house a gunpowder supply that was secretly walled up in one of the basement arches. It was so well hidden that when the British occupied Charleston in 1780–1782, they failed to discover it. During the British occupation, sixty-one citizens were captured and housed in the basement, including Lt. Gov. Christopher Gadsden. This was the beginning of the Provost Dungeon which lies beneath the building.

Another prisoner during this time was a prominent rice planter named Isaac Hayne. Hayne was a state senator, and was originally commissioned as a captain of artillery in the early stages of the American Revolution. When the British seized Charleston in 1780, he was serving in a cavalry regiment. The British offered a pardon and blanket amnesty to all those arrested if they would not serve against the British while they held the city. In 1781, the British changed the terms, and all those that had been paroled and granted amnesty were required to join the royal army or be imprisoned. This was an effort by the British to obtain the cooperation and wealth of Charleston's citizens.

At this point Col. Hayne's wife and children were near death from smallpox, and seeing no other alternative, he agreed to taking the oath of allegiance on one condition: that he not be forced to fight against his former compatriots. This would allow him to remain free to care for his family and also allow him to not impede the patriot cause.

The conditions were agreed upon until patriotic forces began to succeed in areas on the outskirts of Charleston. With Charleston now being faced with attack, the British required all to immediately join the royal army and fight against the rebelling patriot forces. Col. Hayne took this as a breach of agreement and felt that he was released from any obligations to the British. He immediately joined the patriot forces, was commissioned a colonel, and was given a militia company.

Col. Hayne led a successful raid and captured Brig. Gen. Andrew Williamson. British commander of Charleston Col. Nisbet Balfour sent forth a rescue party and successfully intercepted Col. Hayne and his men. Because of his previous oath Col. Hayne was tried by the British, court-martialed, and sentenced to hang. This was to be an example to all that took up arms against the British.

Found guilty of treason, he was marched through the streets of Charleston to the gallows at White Point, where he was hanged. The hanging backfired and had the opposite effect on the citizenry, inspiring them to join the patriot cause, and the British were driven from Charleston in less than a year.

According to legend, as Col. Hayne was en route to the gallows he passed by the home of his sister. She called out to him to return to her and he promised he would. Apparently his boots can still be heard on Broad Street and his apparition haunts the Old Exchange and the Provost Dungeon that he was once housed in.

The dungeon was nothing new to this site. The building was built on the site of the Half-Moon Battery, later known as the Court of Guard. These were razed circa 1767, but not prior to housing some of Charleston's most notorious criminals of that time—pirates. One of the most notorious was Stede Bonnet—known as the "Gentleman Pirate"—and his crew. Bonnet was captured by Col. William Rhett and returned to Charleston on October 3, 1718.

Bonnet's crew was housed in the Guard House at the Half-Moon Battery, but Bonnet was housed in the home of Marshall Partridge. This was a courtesy due to his status as a gentleman. Unfortunately, Bonnet did not take his status as a "gentleman" as well as his captors and he escaped by dressing as a woman. Col. Rhett was once again dispatched to capture Bonnet, and the cross-dressing pirate was returned to his crew. The hanging took place on December 10, 1718, at White Point, now White Point Gardens.

Legend also has it that Stede Bonnet and other buccaneers likewise haunt the Provost Dungeon and sometimes venture up to the Old Exchange Building.

When I was asked to do a book signing, my gracious hosts set up an area in the gift shop. I soon took my position at the small table and prepared to greet customers and sign books as they came to tour the historic location. Not long after I sat down

The Provost Dungeon. *Courtesy of Lost in Legend*

and began the process my pen disappeared. I obtained another and that too soon vanished. The third pen remained on my person the entire time after that and seemed to remedy the lost pen issue.

Just as I sat back down with the third pen several books and a coffee mug came off the shelf behind me. Not only did they come off the shelf, they literally launched themselves. The cup actually hit the floor and shattered some three feet from its original location and about a foot from where I was sitting.

Startled by the noise, I turned and saw what had happened. I was soon joined by several of the workers and I explained to them what had occurred. As they made preparations to clean up the shattered mug I looked at the books that had launched themselves from the shelf. Every one of them were books regarding piracy and pirates. I laughed and told my host that perhaps they were upset that I had never written a book that included pirates. She agreed. At that point I said that if it would make Stede Bonnet happy I would gladly include pirates in my next book.

Apparently it worked and I had no further problems that day.

Stede, I am keeping my promise.

Blackbeard

Chapter 4: Blackbeard's Blockade

32

4

BLACKBEARD'S BLOCKADE

The Day Venereal Disease Caused the Blockade of Charleston Harbor

I grew up in Goose Creek, South Carolina. With a population of approximately 36,000, it is not what I would classify as a small town. We lived in a small, rural subdivision directly across from the gymnasium of Goose Creek High School, home of the Fighting Gators. I ran with the wild boys as much as I could; that is, until my mother removed me from the high school after my freshman year and transferred me to Bishop England High School, a private Catholic school. She hoped that the uniforms and nuns would help me change my wicked ways, and as a matter of fact they did. Instead of being overt and obnoxious I learned to be covert and sneaky. The fact that I ". . . seemed to be doing better . . . ," as she put it, was due to the fact that I was not getting caught near as much.

Little is known of the early life of the man who would become the legendary pirate Blackbeard. The little we do know comes from *The General History of Pyrates*, written by Capt. Charles Johnson in 1724. It tells us that Edward Teach, the man known as Blackbeard, was originally from Bristol, a city in Southwest England. But hundreds of years after he sailed the sea there is still an ongoing debate about who he was and where he came from.

North Carolina historian Kevin Duffus has a much different theory in *The Last Days of Black Beard the Pirate*. He believes that Blackbeard was actually Edward "Black" Beard, the son of Capt. James Beard, and was likely born in Goose Creek sometime around 1690.

Regardless of his early origin, by 1716, a young Blackbeard had joined up with Capt. Benjamin Hornigold in Nassau, Bahamas, in what was known as the Pirates Republic. Hornigold took a liking to the new pirate and soon gave him a sloop of his own to command. The two conducted some very successful raids, and by 1717, two other ships were soon added to their armada. One of the ships was commanded by a new pirate named Stede Bonnet.

Bonnet was a fish out of water among the other pirates. He had been born into wealth on the island of Barbados and had inherited the family estate after his father's death. Around 1709, he married Mary Allamby. The marriage was not what he had expected and his new wife turned out to be a nag and a shrew. Bonnet was so desperate to escape his matrimonial hell that he actually bought a vessel, hired a crew, and with no sailing experience set off to become a pirate.

Bonnet arrived in the Pirates Republic and soon caught the attention of Hornigold and Blackbeard. So Bonnet, with no experience, an aristocratic background, and a pension for fine and frivolous clothing, became known as the "Gentleman Pirate" and joined the armada. And much like Hornigold had done with Blackbeard, Blackbeard took Bonnet under his wing to teach him the fine art of piracy.

By March 1717, the governor of South Carolina had his fill of piracy and sent an armed merchant vessel to the Bahamas to hunt for pirates. Hornigold attacked the vessel in March, causing it to run aground. The captain was able to report that Hornigold had a fleet of five vessels and more than 350 men under his command. By November 1717, Hornigold had captured the French Slave ship *La Concorde de Nantes*. (The ship was originally launched by the Royal Navy in 1710 as *Concord*, but was captured and converted by the French in 1711.) He turned this ship over to Blackbeard, who promptly armed her and renamed her *Queen Anne's Revenge*.

The next venture Hornigold's pirates performed was sloppy, attacking a sloop off the coast of Honduras. As they boarded the ship they were too intoxicated to walk. One of the passengers reported that they caused them no harm other than stealing their hats, because they had gotten drunk the night before and had thrown all of theirs overboard.

Hornigold soon realized his days were numbered as long as his partnership with Blackbeard continued. The arrogance of Blackbeard's antics was attracting far too much attention, especially now that the authorities were dispatching pirate hunters. He dissolved his partnership with Blackbeard and continued piracy on his own until December 1717.

In January 1718, he sailed to Jamaica and received a pardon from the new governor of the Bahamas, Woodes Rogers. Rogers granted the pardon on one condition: Hornigold would become a pirate hunter and turn on his former partners Blackbeard and Stede Bonnet. Hornigold agreed and spent the next eighteen months hunting Blackbeard, Stede Bonnet, and Calico Jack Rackham. Blackbeard's mentor had now become his hunter.

By March 1718, Blackbeard and his flotilla, including Stede Bonnet, had set sail for the harbor at Charles Towne. Along the way they attacked three vessels. They arrived in Charleston Harbor in May and blockaded the port. They immediately captured the pilot boat, and since the town had no guard ship they easily set up a blockade. No ships entered or left the harbor without first being stopped and ransacked by the pirates.

One ship heading for London was the *Crowley*. The ship's passengers included many prominent Charlestonians, including Samuel Wragg and his son. Wragg was a member of the Council of the Province of Carolina. The prisoners were interrogated about the vessels at port and were then locked below deck. The prisoners expected to be ransomed, but the ransom payment was not what they expected. Instead of gold and wealth, the pirates requested something much different.

Blackbeard informed them that his pirates needed medical supplies, and that if they did not receive them he would burn all the ships in the harbor and then execute all of them and send their heads back to the governor. Apparently, during one of their drunken escapades, the armada had incurred an epidemic of syphilis and gonorrhea and they needed treatment. The bizarre ransom demands were made and agreed upon, and one of the *Crowley's* crew (Mr. Marks), along with two of Blackbeard's pirates, were sent to Charleston to collect it.

During those days the treatment for such disease was mercury. At first mercury was used externally as an ointment; the patient was subjected to a complete mercurial rubdown and then isolated in a hot room next to a fire in an effort to sweat out the disease. If the disease did not respond to that treatment, then the mercury was used internally, in most cases in the form of being forced into the opening of the pirate's infected member. It was not unusual for this treatment to go on for years. This gave rise to the saying, "A night with Venus, a lifetime with Mercury." Of course many patients' lifetimes with mercury treatment were rather short and they died of the disease, or from the actual treatment, which caused mercurial poisoning.

The pirates and Mr. Marks were given two days to retrieve the medical supplies and Blackbeard edged his fleet a little closer to Charleston. On the third day, just as Blackbeard was about to start taking heads, a messenger arrived. He had been sent by Mr. Marks to inform Blackbeard that their boat had been capsized and they were delayed. Blackbeard then granted an additional two days.

After the two days the group still had not returned with the supplies, so Blackbeard moved his entire armada of eight ships directly into the harbor, causing a panic in the city. Mr. Marks hastened his return and explained to Blackbeard what had happened. It seems that while he was presenting his demand to the governor and collecting the medication his two pirate escorts had disappeared. He spent the remaining time searching for them and soon located them blind drunk and passed out in a local tavern.

Blackbeard accepted the ransom and released the prisoners minus their possessions. In fact, he stripped the elite of their clothing and sent them back to Charleston in rowboats with severe sunburns.

This sealed his fate with Charleston.

While in Charleston, Blackbeard learned that Woodes Rogers had been given orders to purge the West Indies of pirates. In an effort to lay low and figure out his next move Blackbeard sailed his ships into Beaufort Inlet, off the North Carolina coast. *Queen Anne's Revenge* ran aground on a sandbar. He attempted to save the vessel with the assistance of pirate Israel Hands and his ship the *Adventure*, but his ship also became stuck on the sandbar. Blackbeard abandoned both ships.

Blackbeard had also learned that a royal pardon had been offered to all pirates who surrendered before September 5, 1718. They would receive a pardon for all crimes committed before January 5, 1718, so having just committed the blockade of the Charleston Harbor four months after the caveat, he was not sure if a pardon would be granted. Blackbeard then decided to test the waters by tricking his friend and accomplice Stede Bonnet into surrendering first.

Blackbeard confided in Bonnet that he was aware of the pardon and that he was going to surrender to Governor Charles Eden in Bath Town (Bath, North Carolina). He strongly suggested that Stede Bonnet do the same. He told him that Eden was a man he could trust, and that it was the best thing Bonnet could do. Bonnet immediately left his ship the *Revenge* and took a small sailing boat to Bath Town. Blackbeard had tricked Bonnet into being a guinea pig, and while he was away Blackbeard stripped the *Revenge* of its valuables and cargo and marooned the crew.

Ironically Stede Bonnet was granted the pardon by Governor Eden. When he returned for his ship and learned what Blackbeard had done he became enraged. He adopted the alias Capt. Thomas and set off to seek revenge on his former mentor.

Blackbeard was now being pursued by his mentor and student, and also every pirate hunter commissioned by the governors of the Bahamas and Charleston. So Blackbeard took what he learned from using Bonnet for a test run and also went to Governor Eden and received a pardon. He then took his remaining sloop and sailed into Ocrakoke Inlet and retired . . . sort of. It was not long before he was joined by English pirate Charles Vane. Soon the two attracted the likes of Calico Jack Rackham, Robert Deal, and his former colleague, Israel Hands.

This made Governor of North Carolina Alexander Spotswood very concerned, and soon he sent out pirate hunters of his own. The group included Lt. Robert Maynard of the HMS *Pearl*.

On November 21, 1718, Maynard located the pirates anchored off Ocracoke Island and attacked them. In the ensuing battle Blackbeard was killed. In examining his body, Maynard noted that the pirate had been shot no fewer than five times and had been cut about twenty. The pirate was decapitated and his head was hung from the bowsprit. Blackbeard's body was then thrown overboard, and according to legend swam around the ship three times in an attempt to retrieve his head.

By the following month Stede Bonnet was also dead. Blackbeard's apprentice had given up the quest for vengeance and had returned to piracy. He was subsequently captured and executed. He had managed to escape his initial capture, but was immediately recaptured on Sullivan's Island and hanged in White Point Garden in Charleston on December 10, 1718.

By 1719, Capt. Benjamin Hornigold was also dead. Blackbeard's mentor's ship had encountered a hurricane and was dashed to pieces on a reef close to Mexico. Only five of his men survived.

But what of the legend? Is it true that Charleston's elite were ransomed for a Syphilis outbreak?

On November 21, 1996, exactly 278 years after Blackbeard's death, the wreck of *Queen Anne's Revenge* was located. Since then maritime archaeologists, much like those of South Carolina's Maritime Research Division, have worked to excavate, recover, and catalog artifacts associated with the wreck. Since its discovery over 250,000 artifacts have been recovered and cataloged. Thirty-one cannons have been identified of Swedish, English, and French origin, which would be consistent with a pirate vessel and captured armament. Also among those items recovered were some very interesting additional items, including urethral syringes which were used to administer mercury in the treatment of venereal disease. Also located was a clyster pump used to deliver enemas for quicker absorption.

Since the *Queen Anne's Revenge* was grounded and abandoned to the seas immediately after Blackbeard's blockade, it appears that these items are physical proof that venereal disease did indeed cause the blockade of Charleston Harbor.

Urethral syringe located on the *Queen Anne's Revenge*. Courtesy of North Carolina Department of Natural and Cultural Resources

Edgar Allan Poe

5

THE SEARCH FOR POE'S GOLD

On November 8, 1827, twenty-two-year-old Pvt. Edgar A. Perry arrived at his new post at Fort Moultrie onboard the *Waltham*. After having enlisted in May, he had initially served at Fort Independence, in Boston Harbor, for five dollars a month, but now his regiment was being transferred. Upon his arrival in Charleston he was quickly promoted to "artificer" and his monthly pay was doubled. In this new position the young enlisted man prepared shells for the artillery, and in two years quickly rose to the rank of sergeant major for artillery, the highest rank he could achieve as a noncommissioned officer.

After achieving this rank the young man quickly became bored and disenchanted with military life. He aspired to be a writer, but his first attempt at publication had failed quite miserably. In 1825, he published a poem containing 406 lines which had been edited down to 234. In 1827, he again attempted publication and added additional poems to the first; instead of claiming the material he credited the work simply to "a Bostonian." Only about fifty copies were printed, and it is believed that this failure, accompanied by being thrown out of college for gambling debts, had driven the young man to join the army in the first place.

At this point Sgt. Maj. Perry sought to end his five-year enlistment early, so he revealed his secret to his lieutenant that he was only eighteen at the time of his enlistment and that his real name was . . . Edgar Allan Poe. After his revelation to his lieutenant Poe was forced into an attempt at reconciliation with his foster father. Ironically this resulted in Poe being stuck even deeper in his predicament and receiving an appointment to West Point Military Academy. By the beginning of 1831, Poe desperately wanted out of West Point and the military in general. He was court-martialed, and on February 8, 1831, was discharged after being found guilty of gross neglect of duty, disobedience to direct orders, and refusing to attend classes, church, or formation. Legend has it that he did show up for one formation and wore nothing but his belt, boots, and a smile, but regardless, he got his wish.

During his military career Edgar Allan Poe spent just a little over a year on Sullivan's Island, just on the outskirts of Charleston. The island became the setting for three of his works: "The Balloon Hoax," "The Oblong Box," and most importantly to this tale, "The Gold-Bug." It is also believed that actual events and lost pirate gold inspired Poe to write this tale in which the lead character is bitten by a mysterious gold-colored bug and soon pulls his servant and friend into a quest to decipher a secret message in an effort to find buried pirate treasure.

It is said that Poe initially wrote "The Gold-Bug" at Hampton Plantation during a visit there on military furlough. It is believed that Poe became acquainted with the Rutledge family of Hampton Plantation in McClellanville, South Carolina. This is quite feasible, seeing that Poe and John Henry Rutledge were of the same age and were both born in 1809, just months apart from each other. Both men would inevitably have their meetings with the macabre soon enough, but for now we will stick with Poe.

"The Gold-Bug" was published in 1843, quite some time after Poe escaped from the army. It won a writing contest sponsored by the *Philadelphia Dollar* newspaper. The one hundred dollars Poe received is believed to be the largest sum that he every received for any of his work. It was the most widely read of his works during his lifetime and solidified his position as the father of detective stories and mysteries.

According to authors Geordie Buxton and Ed Macy in *Haunted Harbor*, it is believed that the events of "The Gold-bug" were actually inspired by an incident recorded in the *South Carolina Gazette* in 1735. According to the tale, a Spanish ship was transporting a shipment from Central America back to Spain. The cargo of silver and gold never reached its destination due to the fact that the captain of the ship had met with pirates in St. Augustine and concocted a plan to steal the gold. They agreed to meet off Charleston Harbor in an area now known as the Isle of Palms. They would remove the cargo and bury it, and then the Spanish captain would sail his vessel into Georgetown and scuttle it, leaving the authorities to believe the cargo was lost with the ship. The pirate crew would then pick up the Spanish ship's crew in Georgetown and the two groups would return to the treasure and divide up the spoils. Unbeknownst to them, one of Charleston Harbor's pilot boats had happened upon the two vessels, discovered the plans, and reported what had been witnessed.

Unfortunately a large storm came up in Charleston Harbor and the pirate ship and crew were destroyed by a waterspout off Morris Island. The minimal Spanish crew, with no one to retrieve them, were eventually located hiding in Georgetown and were captured.

Still no one gave up the location of the missing cargo, and unlike Poe's tale it has never been found. Also unlike Poe's tale, this treasure seems to be protected by something a lot more sinister than a colorful insect or a secret code.

A few years after Poe's departure from the military, legend has it that a group of soldiers who were also stationed at Fort Moultrie went in search of the treasure. Their search for buried pirate gold on Morris Island quickly took an interesting turn when they encountered what they described as a ghostly apparition standing watch over the gold.

As the men were staring in disbelief, one of the more brave of the lot began to rapidly approach the apparition. He soon realized that the figure was dressed as a pirate, complete with sword and pistols. As the brave soldier continued his approach the phantom pirate immediately raised his hands above his head and a violent storm began to move in. This did not seem to deter the soldier, who continued to move toward the apparition.

The apparition, seeing that the soldier was not taking the hint, then clapped his hands. When he did the earth trembled and the sands opened up and swallowed the advancing soldier. As expected this had quite the deterrent effect on the other soldiers, who rapidly departed none the richer, but far the wiser, without their cohort.

In July 1863, Francis M. Scott was a young nineteen-year-old soldier assigned to the 62nd Regiment Ohio Volunteer Infantry (OVI) stationed at Folly Beach. The young soldier later wrote an interesting tale about two other members of his unit and their quest for the treasure. His tale, published in 1908, states that another young Union soldier by the name Yokum was assigned to remove any persons living on the island and have them transferred to Port Royal prior to an imminent battle. In doing so Yokum encountered an elderly black woman who told him of six treasure chests that had supposedly been buried by pirates on the island. She also advised him that the chests were buried between two old oak trees in her yard. As she continued her tale, she told him that prior to burying the treasure the pirate captain had murdered one of his own crew members by stabbing him to death, pushed him on top of the chests, and buried him with the gold.

As Yokum was helping the old woman and a child to the boat he stated to her that he supposed that the treasure had long since been found. Much to his surprise, the elderly woman advised him that it had not been retrieved because it was cursed and guarded by the ghost of the murdered pirate. As far as she was concerned the long dead pirate could keep it forever.

Shortly before midnight Yokum advised Lt. Hatcher of the tale, and the two of them left their camp with shovels and lanterns, heading for the two oak trees. It was a windless night, and the two men began digging when they reached the location. As soon as they started digging the wind picked up, the tree tops began to sway, and lightning began to flash as a sudden storm rolled in. As the men continued to dig the storm intensified. Once again lightning flashed, but this time it lingered.

They soon realized that they were no longer alone, for there in the darkness was the clear figure of a pirate watching them as they dug. The men dropped their shovels and ran.

On July 11, 1863, the Union attacked the Confederacy at Fort Wagner. It was a massacre for the Union: 339 Union soldiers died to only twelve of the Confederacy. A week later a second attempt against Fort Wagner was made. This time Col. Robert Gould Shaw led the 54th Massachusetts Volunteer Infantry in an attack against the battery. Although leading them into a massive defeat, he also led them into history, as this unit was comprised entirely of black soldiers. Sgt. William Harvey became the first black Medal of Honor recipient for this battle by refusing to give up the colors or allowing the flag to touch the ground.

In researching this particular legend, it was determined that the two soldiers Moore wrote of in this tale were Aaron D. Yocum and Isaiah Hatcher. Yocum had entered the army in 1862 at age twenty-one and was assigned to the 62nd Regiment OVI. At the time of the incident he would have been a corporal in the unit. Hatcher also entered the army in 1862 at age twenty-four. At the time of this incident he would have been a First Lt. in Company C of the 62nd Regiment OVI, making his ranking consistent with this tale.

Another small group also began their search for the treasure. As their boat approached Morris Island, they soon noticed the skies darkening and the clouds rapidly rolling in toward their location. They ignored the storm, and as they searched the island they too encountered a very large figure. The ghostly apparition drew a long sword and pointed it in their direction. Several of the treasure hunters turned back, but others continued advancing until the figure began to make menacing gestures with the sword and then took up a defensive posture just as the storm struck. At this point all the men raced back to the boat and fled the island as the storm howled around them. The next morning only one of the men was found clinging to the overturned vessel; the rest had perished in the storm. The only survivor provided his rescuers with the tale, but refused to give them the coordinates of his encounter.

In 2014, I was contacted by my friends Sally and Tom Robinson of Charleston Scuba regarding a documentary/pilot video that they were filming with a production company out of Los Angeles, California. I met with the producer and crew members, and learned that this was to potentially be promoted as a possible series involving diving, legends, and the paranormal. I agreed to be the historian for the project and the date was set to start filming.

We set out in to Charleston Harbor with the producer, his crew, a marine biologist, two ghost hunters, the Charleston Scuba crew, and myself. As we toured the harbor Capt. Tom and I were filmed giving local history while the others were filmed diving and speaking on their own fields of expertise. I was still recovering from a dislocated shoulder received during another dive project on the wreck of the *Margaret Scott* so I opted out of the diving part. Tom also piloted the boat.

As we toured the harbor stories of piracy, hangings, death, and disease soon filled the air. We pointed out that Castle Pinckney on the harbor had been a place of execution for many, including soldiers in the 1800s and pirates in the 1700s. In another location we told of the long stretch of Folly Beach that was once known as "Coffin Island." In the 1800s, ships would abandon cholera victims before heading into Charleston Harbor. Sometimes on the return trip they might have stopped and picked them up and buried the dead, but often times they would just leave them behind to die. In 1832, the *Amelia* wrecked off Folly. Twenty of the 120 passengers died of cholera. Charleston quarantined and later abandoned all of them there. When a good-hearted Charlestonian attempted to help them he was beaten to death by other Charlestonians upon his return and the ship and cargo were burned.

In May 1987, several bodies were located buried on the west end of Folly. Of the fourteen bodies located, thirteen were buried facing west. Traditional Christian burial has the deceased facing east so that they may see Christ's return from that direction. Of these thirteen, twelve were missing their heads. All of these bodies were dressed in Union uniforms, and archaeologists soon discovered they were from the 55th Massachusetts Volunteer Infantry Regiment. The missing heads, and the fact they were buried in contrast to traditional methods, are still a mystery. Some attribute it to Confederate bounty hunters, since this unit was also an all-black regiment. Others attribute it to voodoo or root magic. There are others who attribute it to the buried treasure's guardian.

Once Poe and the treasure came up both Capt. Tom and I found ourselves telling the many tales of the missing gold, the pirate ghost, and the hapless folks that chose to ignore the warnings. That was all it took, and we were soon heading toward Morris Island.

Once we got there the ghost hunters realized that they had forgotten their equipment. We exited the boat, shot some footage on the island, and once again began to talk about the treasure. As if on cue the skies began to darken, the wind picked up, and Tom and I cast nervous glances at each other. Getting caught in a storm on the harbor is no laughing matter, and as soon as the lightning began to flash Capt. Tom took control and ordered everyone back to the boat.

As we cast off the storm rolled in. It was soon a race back to the dock through rain and rough waters as the storm pursued us. Interestingly enough, as soon as we docked the storm shifted direction and then stopped. It has always amazed me how quickly that storm came up when the subject matter of buried treasure was mentioned in that location. I am also convinced that Capt. Tom was a lot smarter than our predecessors and did not need to stick around for a ghostly apparition to tell us it was time to go.

The Legare Tomb. *Courtesy of Lost in Legend*

6

THE CURSE OF THE LEGARE TOMB
Setting the Record Straight

Perhaps one of the greatest horrors that any human can experience is to awaken and realize that you have been buried alive. To have your loved ones mourning and grieving your loss, having a funeral, and then placing you in your final resting place in error is probably the worst thing that I can imagine. The mere thought is terrifying, and the horrifying concept of this was not lost on Edgar Allan Poe; a number of his works dealt with it. *Berenice*, published 1835; *The Fall of the House of Usher*, published 1839; *The Black Cat*, published 1843; *The Premature Burial*, published in 1844; and *The Cask of Amontillado*, published 1846, all include the theme of being buried alive.

The event apparently happened more than one would care to think. Epidemics created a need to dispose of bodies quickly, and in some instances perhaps a little too quickly, and folks were still alive.

Duke Ferdinand of Brunswick had such a fear of this happening to him that he designed the first "Safety Coffin." He had a window installed to allow light in, an air tube, and had a lock installed instead of having the lid nailed shut. In his burial shrouds he had a special pocket that contained two keys: one for the coffin and the other for the tomb door. When the former Prussian field marshal and survivor of the Seven Year's War died in 1792, it must have been the real deal, because the exit plan was never initiated.

In 1798, P. G. Pessler, a German priest, suggested that coffins be equipped with a tube in which a rope was contained attached to church bells. The deceased could then ring the church bells if wrongly interred. Obviously this was not a practical concept. Pessler's colleague suggested a trumpet-shaped tube so passing priests could do a sniff test. If you did not stink you got dug up. Again, not really practical.

By the 1820s, a method was worked out with the use of smaller bells, and by 1829, Dr. Johann Gottfried Taberger had designed a system using a cord attached to the corpse's hand, head, and feet, and the other end attached to a bell near a night watchman. Air tubes were later added.

Over three hundred years later folks were still concerned with the issue. In 1995, Fabrizio Caselli invented a coffin with an alarm system, heart monitor, lighting system, and intercom. Still bells and alarms, but now high tech.

Even with three hundred years of preparation, planning, and design, there has not been one recorded incident where any of this has saved a single life. There are many cases where people have indeed been buried alive. In fact, one of the most famous cases involves Margorie McCall in Ireland in 1705. Mrs. McCall died and was buried, only to have grave robbers dig her up and attempt to remove her jewelry by cutting off her fingers. The pain caused her to awaken. I am quite certain that the added smell of would-be robbers suddenly defecating themselves also hastened her awakening. Despite the shock, and a missing finger, Mrs. McCall survived and lived a full life. The second time she died she remained that way, and her stone was engraved with the words, "Margorie McCall – Lived Once, Buried Twice."

I grew up with a tale from Edisto Island, South Carolina, about a child being entombed alive. It was a tale that I horrified little Renee Coker with, and one that I often substituted myself in. Fortunately I escaped time and again, but the child in the legend was not so lucky.

According to the legend, an epidemic swept through the area. Six-year-old Julia Legare developed a fever and became ill. Fever epidemics were not uncommon, and usually killed hundreds when they struck. The diseases were generally transmitted by mosquitoes, but science had yet to make the connection at this point.

Young Julia Legare suffered the same symptoms that young Alice Belin Flagg had faced earlier, and like Alice, Julia soon died. Fear of the disease spreading hastened the need for entombment. The small child was hastily placed in a tomb—the Legare crypt—and the door was sealed.

Two years later, a member of the family was killed in the Civil War and the tomb was opened. Much to the family's horror, the skeletonized body of young Julia was discovered at the door. She had been buried alive. The young child had managed to escape her coffin, only to be trapped by the large stone door. The panicked and frail child had no hope and slowly died inside the dark tomb.

After the family's gruesome discovery every attempt to close the door on the tomb was unsuccessful; it would never stay shut. In fact, the door was chained shut in the 1960s. One day parishioners returned to the church to discover that the door had been ripped from its pins and had fallen inward. In Nell S. Graydon's *South Carolina Ghost Tales* the door is still visible in her photograph of the tomb and the chain is still hanging from the door. By the 1970s, the door had been completely removed and the bodies long since interred in the floor.

The legend states that Julia Legare still haunts the tomb and that it will never remain sealed to this day.

Funny how legends rewrite themselves based on the assumptions of others.

Growing up, I had always heard that the child was a very young boy. I had heard that he belonged to a family of prominence on the island and that he died of Yellow Fever symptoms and was interred in the tomb, and that it was his body that was found when the tomb was later reopened.

When Nell S. Graydon published her story in 1969, she referred to the child as "she." Inside the actual tomb there are three stones. The stones bear the names John Berwick Legare, Hugh Swinton Legare, and Julia Legare. Since Graydon said "she" people assumed the child was Julia.

Funny thing is, Julia married her tomb mate John in 1848 and died in 1852 at age twenty-two. That is a wee bit older than six. She was not the child, nor the ghost that everyone thinks she is.

Julia Georgianna Seabrook married John Berwick Legare in 1848. Julia was part of the very prominent Seabrook family. Together they had a child. He was the other tomb mate, and his name was Hugh Swinton Legare. He died in 1854 at age six. He also died two years after his mother, Julia.

In 1854, a Yellow Fever epidemic struck Charleston; hundreds died as it swept through the Low Country of South Carolina. D. J. Cain actually wrote a medical paper in 1856 about the epidemic entitled, "History of the Epidemic of Yellow Fever in Charleston, S.C., in 1854." He tracked the epidemic back to the steamship *Isabel* arriving from Havana and Key West on May 11. Three days later a passenger was hospitalized with Yellow Fever.

In July, the British ship *Aquatic* was sailing from Cuba when she was quarantined in Charleston with her crew suffering from Yellow Fever. Several other ships later arrived bringing more diseased crew members, and it was not long until the disease reached the shores and the citizens of Charleston.

And it continued to spread. In his paper Cain states:

> The shortest time of exposure to the poison of yellow fever, followed by effect, was somewhat less than two hours. A negro from one of the neighboring islands visited the city, during the course of the epidemic, did not remain quite two hours, returned and died of the fever with black vomit, a few days later.

At that time Yellow Fever was thought to be contagious. We now know it is not. This individual was obviously infected prior to reaching Charleston. Regardless,

Cain's notation verifies that the epidemic had also reached the neighboring islands to Charleston. One of those islands was Edisto.

It was highly likely that little six-year-old Hugh died from the illness. This matches the tale.

Also according to the tale, the skeletonized corpse of the child was not discovered until the tomb was reopened two years later to inter the next body. The next person interred there was Hugh's father, John Berwick Legare. He died two years later.

Quite often researchers discover that Julia died as an adult and they dismiss the tale as an urban legend. The problem is that all the players are listed, it is just that time has confused the actual roles they played. Although no documentation has been located that states six-year-old Hugh Legare died of Yellow Fever in 1854, the probability of such is strong and such documentation is rare. The death of his father two years later also lends credibility to the element of the gruesome discovery.

There is a version of the tale that the senior Legare ran afoul of a hoodoo root doctor on the island and was cursed to see his family perish before him. To have your wife die at a young age and to have your child die two years later possibly entombed alive, only to be discovered after your death two years later, seems to have the elements of a curse, but we will save hoodoo and root magic for another tale.

The first time I visited the tomb, I marveled at just how small it was. I entered the tomb and sat down on the floor. I looked around and watched the spiders and other creepy crawlies moving about the interior, then closed my eyes. I imagined what it would be like to be a six-year-old little boy in complete darkness, panicked and trying to escape.

As a former investigator of child physical abuse and sexual assault cases, I have seen first hand the helplessness in children's eyes as I did my best to protect them and prosecute those that had done them harm. I drew from those experiences, but one thing was different: those kids had hope that someone could help them.

Little Hugh Legare had no hope. Nobody came, and when they did it was too late.

The feeling of horror, fear, and helplessness that this six-year-old child must have felt is unfathomable, and I for one am glad that the tomb remains unsealed.

Fort Sumter

7

THE LUCK OF THE IRISH

The Death of Daniel Hough

The term "the luck of the Irish" dates to the days of the California Gold Rush in 1848. It seems that a majority of the miners discovering gold were Irish. These Irish miners possessed no special skills and no special tools; they just located their fair share of gold by blind stupid luck, thus the term was born. It was a term that has been attributed to the Irish, and the fortunate, ever since.

Not all Irish have the luck, and Daniel Hough was one of them.

Hough was born in 1825, in County Tipperary, in what was then called the United Kingdom of Great Britain and Ireland. After emigrating to the United States, he joined the US Army and became one of more than 150,000 Irishmen to fight for the Union Army during the Civil War . . . well, sort of.

Hough was initially assigned to Battery D of the 1st United States Artillery Regiment. He reenlisted at Fort Moultrie in 1859, and was transferred to Battery E of the same unit, relocating from Fort Moultrie to Fort Sumter in Charleston Harbor.

Following the November 1860 election of Abraham Lincoln as president of the United States, several southern states made declarations of secession from the country. South Carolina demanded that the US Army abandon all of their military facilities in Charleston Harbor.

On December 26, 1860, while the majority of Charleston was recovering from Christmas, Maj. Robert Anderson secretly removed his command from highly vulnerable Fort Moultrie, off of Sullivan's Island, to the more secure and superior Fort Sumter in Charleston Harbor. Charleston considered this an aggressive move, and when the federal authorities attempted to have supplies and reinforcements delivered to Maj. Anderson, the unarmed merchant vessel *Star of the West* was fired upon. On January 9, 1861, the state of South Carolina seized all federal property in the Charleston area except for Fort Sumter, and by February 1861, a new Confederate government was proclaimed.

By March 1861, Lincoln had taken office and considered the Confederacy illegitimate, rejecting the claims of secession. By April 4, 1861, Lincoln had ordered merchant ships to be escorted my military vessels to resupply Maj. Anderson at Fort Sumter. He notified South Carolina Governor Francis W. Pickens of his intent.

Pickens in turn contacted Brig. Gen. Pierre G. T. Beauregard that if the fort was intended to be resupplied by force, Beauregard was to demand its immediate surrender. On April 11, 1861, Beauregard demanded just that and was flatly refused. At 3:20 a.m. the following day, Confederate forces informed Maj. Anderson that their batteries would open fire in one hour. At ten minutes past the hour Capt. George S. James ordered the firing of a single shell, and within moments Edmund Ruffin of Virginia would fire that shell from Fort Johnson toward Fort Sumter, thus starting the American Civil War. By the time the war ended four years later there would be 620,000 lives lost and over 1,100,000 casualties.

In 1861, Edmund Ruffin fired the first shot of the Civil War, and exactly one month after his Confederacy surrendered in 1865 he would fire another shot. This time the shot he fired was into his own head because he refused to accept defeat and declare his loyalty to a reunited United States of America.

Major Anderson held his fire until 7:00 a.m. and the battle continued through the night. The next morning a round ignited the officers' quarters at the fort. By midday the flagstaff had been destroyed, and by 2:00 p.m. Anderson had agreed to a truce. By evening he surrendered the fort. Miraculously no one on either side was killed. The luck of the Irish had smiled down on Daniel Hough, and he, along with his comrades, had survived the first battle of the Civil War relatively unscathed . . . at least for now.

Major Anderson also realized how fortunate they were, and in surrendering the fort he raised the flag again for a final salute. After surviving the thirty-four-hour bombardment Anderson had his soldiers prepare a one hundred gun salute to the flag and the great fort that had protected them. Daniel Hough was assigned to the forty-seventh gun of the salute. His luck soon ran out.

Hough loaded the cannon, and as he was preparing to fire a spark prematurely ignited the charge and the gun exploded. The explosion was so quick and surprising that no one had time to react. The explosion completely tore Hough's right arm off and detonated the ammunition next to the gun. The explosion killed Hough instantly and wounded five others, including Edward Galloway, who would die five days later. The salute was shortened to a fifty guns and Daniel

Cannons of Fort Sumter.
Courtesy of Lost in Legend

Hough's Irish luck had run out. After surviving for thirty-four hours in the first battle of the American Civil War Daniel Hough became the first casualty of the war in a freak accident, ironically by his own hands.

According to legend, the flag was lowered and used to cover the remains of Pvt. Daniel Hough, and there, within the flag, his image was imbedded. Many state scientific reasons for this occurrence, yet others give a more paranormal explanation for the oddity. These folks also believe that having faced the bombardment for so long and coming through unscathed Daniel Hough did not realize he had been killed and continues to haunt the fort. Regardless, the flag does bear an odd image.

Although believed to have been buried at Fort Sumter, the body of Daniel Hough has never been located and the ghost of the first casualty of the Civil War continues to perform his daily duties there, not realizing that he is dead.

On April 14, 1865, exactly four years to the day that Anderson surrendered the fort and lowered the flag, he returned, now a major general, to once again raise the flag as part of a celebration of the end of the Confederacy. President Abraham Lincoln had been invited to this ceremony at Fort Sumter but opted to stay in Washington, DC, and take in the play *Our American Cousin* at Ford's Theater instead. That night, exactly four years to the day that Daniel Hough's luck ran out, so did Lincoln's, when an actor and Confederate sympathizer named John Wilkes Booth entered the president's box, pointed a pistol at his head, and pulled the trigger.

Battle flag with image. *Courtesy of Lost in Legend*

Even at thirty feet underwater there is still no escape.
Courtesy of Lost in Legend

8

I DON'T DO WELL WITH WITCHES

Hex Texting, Maleficium, and the Wreck of the *Margaret Scott*

I do not mix well with witches. I do not mean those that are Wiccan, and are true witches in the sense of what they practice and believe. The true Wiccan practitioners that I have encountered have been quite peaceful, and indeed quite helpful. The Wiccan Rede "An Ye Harm None, Do What Ye Will" assures me that they are far more interested in other things than harming me with *maleficium*.

What is *maleficium* you ask? It is a Latin term for all the evil, malicious, and malevolent sorcery that wicked witches do. It is the casting of harmful spells, or turning folks into toads and other creepy-crawly type of things. It is those types of "witches" that I am talking about. Self-righteous, pious, claiming to have unlimited powers, and trying to intimidate others type of witches. The ones that make you want to drop a house on them or throw a bucket of water on them and watch them shrivel. Those kind of witches.

In 1692, the Salem Witch Trials occurred. It was accusations of *maleficium* that caused Reverend George Burroughs to become the only minister convicted of witchcraft and hanged for his crimes. He was found guilty after accusations were levelled against him by former members of his congregation that had sued him for a personal debt. The damning evidence presented at his trial included testimony that he was able to perform tremendous feats of strength, including lifting a musket by inserting his finger in the barrel. This task could only be accomplished in collusion with Satan himself, and the poor Reverend soon found himself swinging from the end of a noose.

One of the witnesses called to testify against the reverend was John Whilden of Ipswich, Massachusetts.

On June 26, 1696, Reverend William Hubbard of Ipswich wrote to South Carolina Governor John Archdale that a "considerable number" of people wanted to relocate to South Carolina. This letter is believed by many to refer to the Wappetaw community. Over fifty Congregationalists from Ipswich, Massachusetts, including John Whilden, settled fifteen miles north of Charleston, South Carolina, in a community they called Wappetaw. They adopted the indigenous Native American word meaning "sweet water" from the Seewee Indians and thus named the community. It is believed that the entire relocation was based on the fact that they wished to disassociate themselves from New England society because of the witch trials that had taken place in their neighboring town of Salem. It is believed that by 1699, the first church was built.

Today Wappetaw is known as Awendaw, South Carolina, with a population of 1,294 as of the 2010 census. Awendaw was a town created to escape the madness of *maleficium*.

Approximately 161 miles from Awendaw lies the town Winnsboro, South Carolina. In 1792, they faced their own issues with witchcraft.

In Fairfield County many cattle got sick and many people claimed to have been possessed by demonic forces controlled by local witches. A local group called the Gifted Brethren were broken up for practicing hypnosis. One of the founders was tried for heresy in Charleston, found guilty, and hanged.

In Fairfield County, four people were accused of witchcraft, including Mary Ingleman. Mary Ingleman was believed to be between seventy and eighty years old at the time of the incident. According to the Fairfield County Historical Museum, an account of the case was published in the *South Carolina Gazette* on November 10, 1792.

A large group of townsfolk gathered together, formed a lynch mob, and held their own trial on a farm outside town. John Crossland appointed himself to preside over the case. As testimony was heard Rosy Henley accused Mary Ingleman of putting a spell upon her and her sister and causing them to levitate. According to the testimony four strong men were unable to pull the frightened women back to Earth. Martha Holly Willingham also testified that she had been levitated and was also afflicted with spitting up hairballs with pins sticking out of them.

Adam Free also testified against Mary Ingleman. Interestingly enough, Free was her own son from a previous marriage. Free accused her of causing one of his cows to levitate in the air and then fall to the ground, snapping its neck. Free's son, Jacob, testified that she had turned him into a horse.

Another witness, Isaac Collins, claimed that she also turned him into a horse and then rode him six miles to an apple orchard to attend a "grand convention of witches." There Satan himself complimented Mary Ingleman on the fine steed to which she responded that it was "that rascal Collins."

Mary Ingleman and the other accused were found guilty and bull whipped. They then had their feet held to a fire until the soles burst open. Apparently this was deemed adequate punishment and they were released. As Mary Ingleman made her way through the woods she was again assaulted by another party who beat her, threw her to the ground, and pinned her by her neck with a large pine log. She was left to die but managed to escape.

Other versions of the tale state that after she escaped this ordeal she was again captured by a third party and hanged. Once again she cheated death; after the party left her to strangle slowly the rope broke.

Mary Ingleman sought justice for her ordeal and was able to get the judge and Reverend William Yongue to issue a warrant for John Crossland, who had acted as judge, jury, and executioner in her trial. Crossland was found guilty of aggravated assault and fined ten pounds sterling and costs. He never paid his fine and left town after his trial.

Mary Ingleman attempted to bring justice against many others in the town but was unsuccessful. She suffered in pain and bore the scars from the whipping and burning until her death. This was the price of accusations of *maleficium*.

But that was not the end of Mary Ingleman. It is said that she continues to haunt the Fairfield County Courthouse, seeking justice against those who have already faced eternal justice centuries ago. It is said that many people have seen an elderly woman sitting on the courthouse steps. As they approach they are shocked, as they notice the whip scars still visible on her arms, and she slowly fades away.

My negative experiences with witches and *maleficium* started several years ago, when I became involved with one on a project I was asked to look into. Since the party involved has passed into the great beyond I feel that I can share the tale without retaliation from her, at least in this world.

This union was not of my own making, believe me. She was invited along by a well-intentioned resident who was apparently not overly enthused about my systematic approach to their paranormal problem.

It all started when I heard of a local subdivision that was experiencing paranormal activity after developers had disturbed a slave cemetery while clearing lots on the property. I was contacted and sent several e-mails that included story after story of paranormal activity, poltergeist activity, and ghostly sightings. I was intrigued yet skeptical. Many of the homeowners had experienced ghostly sounds, such as banging and knocking. Others had heard disembodied voices. Yet others had seen shadowy figures moving about in their residences.

Frankly, I do not consider myself a ghost hunter, but the property had once been an old plantation, and I had grown up hunting and fishing there with my father and brothers. I had fished the ponds there with my mother and siblings, and I still to this day can see my mother slipping and falling down an embankment and sliding down into the pond. My sister was concerned about Momma, but my brother and I were more concerned about the large splash ruining our fishing hole for the day. Yup, I had a great love for the area, and was saddened to hear that yet another site of many of my childhood memories had been sold to developers.

The tales that the residents were speaking of also sounded a little too familiar, and I felt that perhaps far too many of the homeowners were drawing on childhood memories; like myself, they had grown up with Carol Anne staring at her television set and announcing, "They're here." after moving into a home built over a cemetery. I strongly suspected that it was nerves, overactive imaginations, and memories from the motion picture *Poltergeist* that prompted these experiences. I also hoped . . . just to be on the safe side . . . that there were no clown toys around with an inclination for hiding under beds.

I began looking into the matter, but pretty soon the person that had asked me to research the issue invited—and I quote—"a Psychic Witch." From the start we did not hit it off. She kept trying to get a "read" on me, and attempted to delve into my personal life through interrogation. She also wished to learn as much as she could about my research on the location *before* I told anyone else about it. I do not have any problems sharing information with anyone that I work with on a joint effort, but I took this as an indication that she was wanting me to furnish her with my research so she could in turn impress others with her "psychic" abilities. I clammed up on the information sharing in this case, except for a little bit of false information that I provided her with to see what she would do with it. If I was right, she would use it to impress the residents. If I was wrong and she was truly psychic, she would know the information was bogus and she would tell me such. No harm no foul.

I will give you one guess what happened.

She did not fare so well on the psychic testing. During one of her psychic readings she became impatient and used all the bogus information I had given her to impress one of the homeowners. Problem is, the homeowner was already aware of what I was doing and knew the information was phony. After the reading I met with the psychic witch and the homeowner and we confronted her. The issue was not that we were just wanting to be hateful and mean. The issue was that she had used the false information in an effort to "prove" her abilities so that she could begin charging these folks in the neighborhood for her time at about $65.00 an hour.

She was not happy and turned on me, since I was a "non-believer" and it was all my fault. I informed her that this was all her fault, and that if she was truly psychic she would have known from the start that I thought she was full of crap, she never would have wanted to work with me, and she would not have been along for two days harassing me. At this point I took my research and recused myself from the project.

Well, the psychic witch was not done. She immediately began to call and harass me. She then began to text me. When I ignored it the *maleficium* started. She then began to cast evil spells upon me by text. I believe that I am the first historian and researcher to ever be hexed by text, or "text hexed." In *maleficium* I do not think hex texting is allowed, and I do not know if it is still illegal. I do know that harassment in South Carolina is definitely illegal, so law enforcement soon became involved.

There is a bright side: at least it was not a sex hex text. I can think of nothing scarier than receiving a curse *and* a naked picture of that particular being.

As I suspected, law enforcement soon determined that she was more a con artist than a witch, but she quickly solidified my position on never working with wicked witches again.

Well I was wrong, and that brings us to the *Margaret Scott* and more *maleficium*.

In March 2014, I was contacted by Ashley Deming of the Maritime Research Division and asked if I would be interested in assisting with a survey of the Stone Fleet in Charleston Harbor. I had worked with MRD on a number of projects, and had even taken both phases of their field school to learn their methods and become a volunteer research diver with them. I jumped at this chance. MRD's goal was to survey and record the remains of the great Stone Fleet, but Lost in Legend's interest was in just one of the ships: the wreck of the *Margaret Scott*.

For those unfamiliar with the Stone Fleet, it was actually a group of ships purposefully sunk in Charleston Harbor during the Civil War. The fleet consisted of a number of derelict vessels that were loaded with stone and brought in to Charleston Harbor by Union forces during the war in 1861 and 1862. They were deliberately sunk in certain sections of the harbor in an attempt to obstruct the waterways and keep Confederate blockade runners from getting supplies to Southern forces. Over forty vessels were utilized, including a ship called the *Tenedos*, which a young sailor by the name Herman Melville once traveled on. It would prompt him to write a poem about the ship and all the others in that doomed derelict fleet entitled, "The Stone Fleet."

The project started in March in the bitter cold. At this point operations consisted of remote sensing using side scan sonar and magnetometer sweeps looking for images consistent with a decomposed wreck. Unlike the pristine wrecks displayed on documentaries located hundreds of feet below the surface in cooler waters, the wrecks of the Stone Fleet were long destroyed by the murky, warm, and shallow waters of Charleston Harbor, and at a depth of thirty feet consisted of little more than stones that had once filled them and the metal fasteners that had once held them together.

Remote sensing was a long, cold, and miserable process, and in fact before the research boat hit the water it had started snowing. Of course there was no accumulation, but it was a sign of things to come. On the first run it was so cold that Brown Pelicans were landing in the boat and sitting on the twin motors in an effort to stay warm. For the next two months myself, MRD, and other divers would miserably ride up and down the harbor, dragging equipment and taking readings in an attempt to locate targets to dive on in warmer months. I could not wait for May, warmer weather, and the diving part of this project to commence. I also wanted my shot with the *Margaret Scott*.

The *Margaret Scott* was a 330 ton barque rigged ship purchased from the US marshall in New Bedford, Connecticut, after having been confiscated as a slave ship. It was loaded with stone and was sank in Maffitt's Channel, off Charleston Harbor, on January 20, 1862. There was nothing extraordinary about this vessel other than its namesake, for legend has it that this particular ship was named after Margaret Scott, a woman executed in the Salem witch trials in 1692. A ship sunk at sea named after a witch—the sea witch!

Aye, and a truer nickname has never been given.

> SEVENTY-SEVEN-YEAR-OLD MARGARET SCOTT WAS A PRIME CANDIDATE FOR THE CITIZENS OF ROWLEY, MASSACHUSETTS, TO COME AGAINST. SHE HAD GIVEN BIRTH TO SEVEN CHILDREN AND MOST DIED AT BIRTH. OTHERS DIED IN CHILDHOOD, AND ONLY ONE CHILD—A MALE—MADE IT TO ADULTHOOD IN THE TOWN. HER HUSBAND WAS DEAD, AND SHE HAD BEEN A WIDOW FOR TWENTY-ONE YEARS. THIS CAUSED HER TO BECOME A BEGGAR, WHICH OF COURSE MADE HER AN OUTCAST IN THE COMMUNITY.
>
> NOW ACCUSED OF WITCHCRAFT, THE EXACT CHARGES AGAINST HER WERE FOR "SPECTRAL IMAGERY" AND "MALEFICIUM." OUT OF THE SIX ACCUSERS PRESENTING DEPOSITIONS AGAINST HER IN THIS TRIAL, FOUR WERE YOUNG LADIES WHO TESTIFIED THAT SCOTT APPEARED TO THEM IN A SPECTRAL IMAGE AND ATTACKED THEM. THE OTHER TWO ACCUSERS TESTIFIED OF MALEFICIUM—THAT SHE HARMED THEIR CROPS AND LIVESTOCK, RESULTING IN A BAD HARVEST, LIVESTOCK BEHAVING STRANGELY, AND A COW DYING. THE TRIAL LASTED ONE DAY; MARGARET SCOTT WAS FOUND GUILTY OF WITCHCRAFT AND EXECUTED BY HANGING ON SEPTEMBER 22, 1692.

May 22, 2014, finally rolled around, and it was my turn to dive on the project. In contrast to the frigid weather of earlier months, the Pelicans kept their distance and we enjoyed warm weather as we motored out. We soon reached our destination and suited up over the first stop, the *Margaret Scott*. My dive partner entered the water first. The surface was a bit choppier than usual, but

A barque rigged ship similar to the *Margaret Scott*

not anything I had not been in before. I finished making last minute adjustments with my gear and was going over a safety check with the dive master before doing a back roll off the boat. At the last minute I switched my camera over to a hook on the left side of my BCD (Buoyancy Compensator Device) vest and initiated the roll. The last minute camera re-positioning turned out to be a very, very bad mistake.

The goal of a safety check is to insure that all equipment is functioning and properly positioned. The intended goal of the back roll is to get the diver away from the boat and into the water when conditions are not ideal for a standing entry. My last minute repositioning of the camera defeated both, for as I rolled backward, the dangling camera caught on the inside gunnel wall of the boat and the strap kept me momentarily dangling off the side of the boat as it rocked back and forth on the waves.

I remained dangling there for what seemed like an eternity until a larger wave hit us, the boat rolled, and the camera strap snapped, sending me into the water directly beside the boat. The force sent the camera ricocheting off the deck and into the extra dive tanks on the opposite side and sent me sliding upside down along the side of the boat.

As I was suspended over the water, I remember thinking, "this is not going to be good." As I fell beside the boat, I knew I was in trouble and entirely too close. As I hit the water, righted myself, and surfaced I saw the boat rolling down on top of me. I was being pulled under it as it rolled on the waves. Fortunately I had not fully inflated my BCD and was not completely under the boat. The edge of the boat struck my tank, and that is the last thing I remember, as I recall being knocked under water and resurfacing behind the boat. I was a bit dazed and decided I needed to abort this effort and check my equipment for damage, so I fully inflated my BCD. I then took one stroke back toward the boat with my right arm and then attempted one with my left. I was instantly overcome with the greatest pain I have ever felt in my entire life. It was disorienting and actually caused me to drop my regulator from my mouth. My whole left side of my body was on fire. I did not know if I had been struck by the propeller, bitten by a shark, or was somehow being electrocuted. In nanoseconds all these thoughts flashed through my mind.

Back on the boat, archaeologist and diver Nate Fulmer could see that there was a problem, which was soon verified by me dropping my regulator, swallowing a mouthful of salt water, and coughing. He yelled to me to put my regulator back in as the team prepared the boat for a rescue as I was drifting away on the waves. The problem was that while cranking up the boat would be beneficial to my rescue, the fact was my partner was also in the water, his location was unknown, and a churning propeller could become fatal should he resurface.

As soon as Nate yelled I replaced my regulator and training kicked in. I rolled over on my back and began kicking toward the boat. My left arm was completely useless and I was in excruciating pain. Then adrenaline kicked in. I was on my back kicking and I overshot the boat. As the sudden burst of energy wore off a line was tossed and I was pulled around to the back of the boat. Exhausted, I climbed the ladder and laid across the gunnel of the boat. Ashley leaned over me and removed my fin as I bent my knee for her to reach it. As the boat rolled on the waves she slipped and fell on top of me and all I can remember at that point was a flash of brilliant white light and what felt like ice flowing through my body. The next thing I remember is being on the bottom of the boat with Nate administering oxygen, Ashley calling in information, and my dive partner Jim Spirek back on the boat. I do not know how or when they recovered him, but our skipper, Joe Beatty, was speeding off to meet the rescue boat.

Since I was unable to speak and the pain was radiating from my left shoulder across my chest the team thought I was experiencing a heart attack. The team, and later the paramedics, treated me as such, but after removing the upper part of my wetsuit the pain seemed to move from my chest and back into my shoulder. By the time I had reached the emergency room the pain had lessened. I do not know if it had actually lessened or I had become more delirious from it, but at this point I began finding everything hysterical.

As they wheeled me in half naked in a wetsuit with a dive knife still strapped to my leg I began cracking jokes and making smart aleck comments. As we passed by other patients and staff, I realized that folks were looking at this injured diver strapped to a gurney, so I started stating very loudly, "I know what I saw and I am telling you that I am sure that it was a great white shark at least twenty feet long!" Obviously it was not a shark, but the reaction from others in the hospital was priceless. Frankly, I thought my paramedics were going to turn my gurney over laughing.

Doctors soon discovered the issue; when the boat glanced off my tank it struck my left shoulder, dislocating it. As I attempted to swim with that shoulder I proceeded to tear my rotator cuff. When Ashley crawled across me on the boat she slipped and fell on top of me and inadvertently reset my shoulder in the process. The tight wetsuit had compressed the injury and distributed the pain across my chest. Once the arm was reset and the upper portion of the wetsuit was removed the pain lessened a bit.

It took a year to recover, but had it not been for my own training, a quick response from the Maritime Research Division, and a little luck, I may not have survived at all.

Or perhaps hex texting actually works . . .

Sheriff James McTeer

ROOT MAGIC
Paint, Police, and a Hoodoo Showdown

"Have you ever heard of Haint Blue?" my friend Tom Rabon asked as he was preparing to mix some paint per a phone order from a customer. "As a matter of fact I have," I responded, but I do not suspect he expected that answer or the thirty-minute lecture on Gullah folklore and root magic he was about to receive.

During the time of slavery the enslaved, although deprived of their freedom, managed to preserve their West African history, folklore, and culture. They passed this on to their descendants, who continue to keep those traditions alive to this day. The terms "Gullah" and "Geechee" are used to define the cultures that those slaves brought with them to the coastal regions and Sea Islands of South Carolina. This also included their own variety of ghosts, ghouls, and goblins, and the magic used to summon them and repel them. This is what is known as hoo doo or root magic.

I first became acquainted with root magic as a young deputy sheriff in the mid-1980s. While searching a prisoner, I discovered moss in the individual's ears—Spanish moss to be exact. He had been told by a root doctor that this would prevent evil spirits from communicating with him. He believed in it to the point that there would have been a confrontation had I attempted to remove it. A very wise chief jailer asked if he could inspect the conjurer's work, and after doing so determined that it was not contraband and allowed the prisoner to keep it. Not long after that incident I made an arrest, and as I searched this prisoner I discovered a small cloth bag containing a red powder. As I opened up the bag and began inspecting the powder the individual immediately became fearful and agitated. He soon became combative. Once again, the wise old chief jailer intervened, and after field testing it to make sure it was not an illegal narcotic it was returned to the prisoner. I later learned that it was a talisman to protect the individual from sickness and death, and by tampering with it I could have inadvertently reversed the spell and killed the individual. So powerful was the prisoner's belief in this root magic that he would have killed me first.

As my career took me to another agency and deeper into areas such as James and Johns Island, Kiawah and Seabrook Island, and also Edisto Island, my encounters with the mysterious and supernatural side of the Gullah culture continued and became more frequent. Soon myself and others were addressing issues of hexes and hauntings along with armed robberies, burglaries, and assaults. There were also times that the lines blurred and blended, such as when my friend Rick Presnell was called out to a vandalism on an elderly woman's property and ended up placing a spell of protection on her home.

Individuals had painted an animal skull, attached feathers to it, and placed it on the woman's porch. This was most probably some of the island kids harassing the old woman due to her beliefs and it obviously worked. She thought that someone had cursed her, or as they say *put the root on her*. You see, she was not as upset at the idea of the individuals returning as she was the evil spirits that guided them. Rick reassured the emotionally distraught old woman and told her that he knew how to handle such things and that he would take care of it. He left the home, went to the local grocery, and purchased two bags of rock salt. He then returned to the residence to pour a circle of rock salt around the entire house. He also poured salt at every window, door, and threshold he could find. It was a barrier evil spirits could not cross, and it would protect her home until she could repaint the thresholds Haint Blue. This seemed to do the trick and the elderly woman never called again.

In working the island areas, we noticed that a lot of doors, thresholds, windows, and shutters were painted a particular shade of blue. This was a sky blue with just a tinge of green to it. I soon discovered that even the Presbyterian church on Edisto Island had the ceiling to the front porch painted this color. The church was founded in 1685, and the current church was built in 1830, so I was quite certain that the color had a lot to do with the area and the culture there on Edisto Island. Upon inquiring I soon learned that this shade was known as Haint Blue, and it was used to repel ghosts . . . or haints, as the Gullah folks called them. I was also told that the blue confused nesting insects, such as wasps; they would not build their nests on the blue porch, thinking that it was open sky.

Law enforcement and dealings with the supernatural are nothing new to South Carolina. Adam Meek was sheriff in York County from 1791–1797, and during his tenure he received a report of a phantom haunting a roadway near Bullocks Creek. The roadway cut across a field known as Gordon's Old Field. The apparition appeared at dusk and greeted all that attempted to cross the field.

It seemed the apparition was bound by the field, and those that did encounter him were relieved upon discovering that as soon as it reached the wood line surrounding the field the phantom would disappear. Eventually one of Meek's neighbors had an encounter and informed him of it. "What did it say?" Meek inquired. The neighbor reluctantly informed the sheriff that he did not allow it to get close enough to converse. Meek advised the neighbor that he would find out what it wanted.

Soon after being advised of the issue Sheriff Meek rode out to the field and did indeed encounter the apparition. He stopped his horse at the edge of the field, dismounted, and walked toward the apparition. The apparition soon met him in the field, and the two began conversing while walking the 200-yard field. When they reached the end of the field the phantom disappeared. Sheriff Meek then returned to his horse and departed.

Sheriff Meek never revealed what the spirit had told him. Many feel he had promised the apparition that he would attend to some of the ghost's unfinished business, because immediately upon returning home the sheriff packed some belongings and disappeared for almost two months. Apparently, whatever the sheriff did appeased the ghost because he was never seen again. Sheriff Adam Meek may have been the first South Carolina sheriff that went above and beyond the call of duty in dealing with the supernatural, but he was definitely not the last. Another sheriff became a practicing root doctor to combat another in his community.

James McTeer became the youngest sheriff in United States history when he became sheriff of Beaufort County in 1926 at age twenty-two. He finished out his father's term when his father died two years into his term after being re-elected in 1924. Sheriff James McTeer would remain sheriff of Beaufort County, South Carolina, for the next thirty-seven years, but because of necessity he would soon also become a practicing root doctor for the next fifty years.

McTeer first became acquainted with root magic at a young age, but his first encounter with it in a law enforcement application occurred when he was a very young man delivering dinner to a couple trustees of his father's. Trustees are prisoners that have minor charges and are entrusted to perform work details. These two were entrusted with caring for horses and tracking dogs. McTeer was bringing them their dinner one night when he encountered a strange incident between the two individuals and one of his father's deputies.

Deputy White had discovered the two men had been slipping out the gate after dinner at night and seeing their lady friends instead of doing their work detail. The deputy allowed them to eat dinner, and then, as he prepared to leave, he turned around and informed the trustees that he was aware of what they had been doing. At this point he removed a small jar of powder from his pocket and poured the contents in the gate's opening. The white powdery cross stood out brightly against the dark earth. He advised them that he had gone to Root Doctor Buzzard, who had prepared the powder, and they could walk out that gate that night if they wanted, but once they crossed that powder they would never walk again. They never slipped out again until their time was served.

After becoming sheriff McTeer soon learned that the area was divided into sections, and much like drug cartels each had a leader that ran a particular section. Dr. Crow, a.k.a. Alliston Hamilton, ran the Burton area, while Dr. Bug, a.k.a. Peter Murray, ran the Broad River area. There were lesser doctors, such as Dr. Hawk and Dr. Snake, but Dr. Buzzard was encroaching on all of them, and was soon to become the hoo doo godfather of Beaufort County.

Dr. Buzzard was actually Stepheny Robinson, and was about fifty years old when he reached the height of his power. He was known for his purple-tinted sunglasses, which became his trademark that many others soon copied. Dr. Buzzard's father was a root doctor who was allegedly a descendant of a powerful African root doctor. The elder had taught the latter all that he knew, and soon Stepheny Robinson began practicing and adopted his father's name, Dr. Buzzard.

Dr. Buzzard became extremely successful as a root doctor, and likewise became financially successful. He owned his own home, several big and expensive cars, and even financed and built the two largest churches on St. Helena's Island.

Dr. Buzzard had risen to prominence in the area for a feat he used to impress the local population. Through intimidation and bribery he had the assistance of three law enforcement officers. He had convinced them that he would put a hex on them if they did not comply and he had a coffin delivered to the jailhouse. He then climbed into the coffin and told them to chain it shut. At first the men were afraid that they would inadvertently kill the doctor by suffocation, but he assured them that just like none of the cases they ever brought against him were airtight, neither was the coffin. He again threatened them and they did his bidding. From inside the coffin he told them that he would be out and home before they finished dinner.

The men secured the locks on the coffin and then secured the building as they left. They went down the street to a local restaurant for dinner. After finishing, they returned to the jail and unlocked the door. Much to their surprise, all the chains and locks were lying in a pile on the floor. When they removed the lid they were both startled and terrified when a black cat screamed and jumped out at them. Dr. Buzzard had escaped, and had instantly taken reign as the "Hoo Doo Godfather of Beaufort County."

Sheriff McTeer believed that root doctors dealt mainly with auto-suggestion in an individual's subconscious mind. He also had an issue with them practicing medicine without a license, obtaining goods under false pretenses, and fraud. They also empowered and emboldened others to break the law, and often interfered with investigations and intimidated witnesses. McTeer tried many times to make a case against Dr. Buzzard but always ended up falling short.

One day McTeer and his men captured a young burglary suspect. As McTeer was searching him he discovered a small vial containing a yellow liquid. As he inspected it the prisoner became very emotionally distraught and told him it was a talisman for protection. He said that he had purchased the vial from Dr. Buzzard for $100.00 and was told that if he showed it to anyone or told them about it the medicine would reverse its magic and kill him.

McTeer, thinking quickly, told him that obviously he was stronger than Dr. Buzzard's magic because he had seen it, been told about it, and the owner was still alive. The logic worked, and McTeer then began to use it to create a case against Dr. Buzzard for obtaining money under false pretenses and practicing medicine without a license.

Sheriff McTeer sent a deputy out to pick up Dr. Buzzard. As soon as Dr. Buzzard entered the sheriff's office he turned and stared at the young burglar through his purple-tinted glasses. Immediately the young man began beating his legs as if being bitten by fire ants. He broke into a sweat and began moaning, then fell out of his chair. His eyes rolled back in his head and he began frothing at the mouth. Sheriff McTeer soon found himself telling the young man that he would not have to testify and that no charges would be brought against Dr. Buzzard.

"Are we done here?" asked Dr. Buzzard. McTeer responded that one day he was going to find a spell that would work on Dr. Buzzard. Dr. Buzzard responded, "You do your job and I'll do mine," as he was being escorted out. The young man's seizures soon subsided after Dr. Buzzard left.

Not long after this incident Sheriff McTeer learned that Dr. Buzzard was getting paid to "chew the root" on him and other court officials. Dr. Buzzard was accepting money to sit in the courtroom and chew on a root while a bond hearing, trial, or sentencing was going on. If the person was found not guilty Dr. Buzzard's fame skyrocketed. If the person was found guilty then Dr. Buzzard explained that the sentence would have been far greater had he not been there. It was a win/win for the conjurer and he made a fortune.

One day a bailiff discovered a white powder on the judge's bench. He also discovered it on the solicitor's and sheriff's tables. Sheriff McTeer scanned the courtroom and soon located Dr. Buzzard. He approached the conjurer and advised him that he could chew root all day long until his teeth fell out and his gums bled, but if he ever put hex powder on their desks again he would send him to jail for sixty days. The root doctor apologized and said he would make it right, and the next day the sheriff found two live white chickens caged on his porch.

Sheriff McTeer felt the root doctors were dangerous and posed a significant threat to those that believed in them and utilized them. This was soon to be proven the case with Dr. Bug.

During World War II, many of the men were being rejected for medical reasons when they showed up at the draft board. Time and time again these men were being rejected for heart irregularities. Soon there were too many to be a coincidence and Sheriff McTeer was contacted. He soon learned that the men were being given a potion by Dr. Bug and were paying extravagantly for it.

Sheriff McTeer and two FBI agents soon paid Dr. Bug, a.k.a. Peter Murray, a visit. Upon executing a search warrant they discovered a trunk containing over $3,000 in cash, another trunk with an assortment of small bottles, and a small bag containing a substance that was soon determined to be arsenic.

Investigation revealed that Dr. Bug had been dipping his pen knife in the arsenic and mixing it in a glass of moonshine. He then instructed the men to return to him for several treatments. The arsenic did indeed induce heart irregularities, and Dr. Bug had succeeded in saving many of the young men from dying in war by simply poisoning them here instead. He was actually so proud of his accomplishments he made a full spontaneous confession. He was charged with administering poison and convicted at trial. After Dr. Bug died in prison and Dr. Crow died, Dr. Buzzard reached the height of his power and seized both their territories.

Sheriff McTeer soon had his hands full dealing with the spells that Dr. Buzzard was dealing out. One day the Sheriff was at magistrate's court and had to deal with a man desiring to take a warrant out against another for harassing him with bad root magic. McTeer soon learned that the man believed that Dr. Buzzard had put the hex on him and that he had gone to Dr. Buzzard to take the hex off, but the talisman had failed. McTeer suggested that Dr. Buzzard was playing both men for additional money.

He asked the man the ingredients of the concoction and immediately told him that Dr. Buzzard had deliberately left out the key ingredient, *asophedita* or stinkfinger root. Of course he was making this up, but the man did as he was instructed and the feud ended. Soon the man was singing the praises of the new root doctor, Sheriff McTeer, and others began coming to him for help. He told them that he was a Christian and could only use his root magic for good and take off hexes, otherwise it would reverse on him and harm him. He was soon being called the "White Prince" or "White Doctor" instead of sheriff.

One day a friend came to the sheriff and advised him that a middle-aged woman that had worked for him believed she had been hexed by Dr. Buzzard and would not even leave her bed. Sheriff McTeer went with the man and discovered that the woman had been in bed for well over a month and was slowly dying because of her fear. Angered by what he saw, he concocted a plan. He advised the man to tell the woman that McTeer was a root doctor, but needed assistance from Dr. Hawk, and that he would pay whatever it took to make her better. The ill woman took comfort in this.

Dr. Hawk owed McTeer a favor; McTeer had captured a robbery suspect who had robbed Dr. Hawk's store. McTeer had Dr. Hawk create a red root concoction and the two then went and buried it that night by the woman's front porch. The next day he sent word out that very evening he and Dr. Hawk were going to remove the hex.

That evening, the two arrived to a very large crowd. They had even brought the woman and her bed into the yard. As McTeer stood watch, Dr. Hawk cut a switch from a peach tree and coiled it up in his hand like a spring. He then uttered unintelligible words over it and released the spring. It soared through the air and landed at the front porch exactly where they had buried the concoction the night before. Dr. Hawk ran to the spot, dropped to his knees, and began frantically digging. He soon uncovered the evil root, held it up high, and screamed for everyone to get back because it was a death root.

As fear engulfed the crowd and they backed away Dr. Hawk screamed. The sight of this huge, hulking man screaming created absolute terror, and he jumped to his feet and ran as hard as he could down to the river and threw the offending concoction in. He slowly returned, sweating and exhausted, and declared that the curse was over. The woman sat up in bed, much to the amazement of the crowd, and Dr. Hawk advised them that this was done because McTeer was more powerful than Dr. Buzzard, and he was only able to do the job because McTeer had shown him what to do. In essence what just happened was a known root doctor had declared that McTeer was more powerful than the most powerful root doctor, and that he was so powerful he had taught a lesser conjurer how to defeat it. This not only set McTeer up as an equal to Dr. Buzzard, but it showed that he could defeat him.

Of course the news soon got back to Dr. Buzzard, and he threatened McTeer by telling the believers to carry him a message that they would soon see who was stronger. McTeer sent back a message to tell Dr. Buzzard that trouble was very close to him.

As fate would have it, tragedy struck. Dr. Buzzard's son was driving his father's vehicle when he ran off a causeway into a river and the young apprentice drowned. A few days later a very distraught Dr. Buzzard showed up at Sheriff McTeer's home with two white chickens. He wanted a truce. McTeer had beaten the root doctor by trickery and a horribly cruel twist of fate.

McTeer saw the great sadness in the man's eyes. He made him promise not to provide any more medicine or perform any illegal acts. Dr. Buzzard agreed. Then much to McTeer's surprise, Dr. Buzzard asked McTeer to become his apprentice so he could pass on the family tradition that had just ended with the death of his son. McTeer agreed and became a practicing root doctor for half a century.

When preparing this book, I took a road trip to Beaufort with professional photographer Jon Jackson. He was working on a separate project, and I decided to tag along for the day and get some shots for this book. One of the locations was Sheriff McTeer's grave.

We arrived at the church, and both Jon and I searched the graveyard to no avail. At this point we entered the church to inquire from the docent there if he knew where the grave was located. He did not, but gave us directions to a woman who would know. We exited the church and once again stopped in the graveyard and had a discussion as to how we were going to proceed.

We decided to continue searching when all of a sudden an elderly black gentleman walked up off the street. He told us that he could help us find anyone in the graveyard. This was an unsolicited response and quite shocking. He also advised us that he was former Army and showed us a military ID listing his former rank as corporal. When I could get a word in edgewise with the corporal I asked him where Sheriff McTeer was. He responded "across the street" (in another section) and he gave us directions. He did not have a lot to say about Dr. Buzzard and avoided questions regarding him. We gave him a few dollars for his information and he disappeared as quickly as he had appeared.

Jon and I followed the directions of our bizarre impromptu guide and arrived at the marker. Like the other markers in the graveyard, McTeer's had dirt splattered up from the ground all over the lower half. Unlike the other markers, it had a red powder all over the upper half. It was the only marker in the graveyard bearing red powder.

I concluded it was root magic. From McTeer's own memoirs he wrote that red powder was to ward off sickness or death. Jon stated that he had a brush back in the SUV that would get the dust off for some better photos. I declined the offer.

Still shaking my head at the bizarre probability of a homeless vet with pertinent information showing up at the precise minute we needed it and wondering what good root had befallen us, I sure did not want to take any chance of creating any bad root by brushing off the powder.

I do not know who you are that placed it there, but here's to your health.

James McTeer's grave. *Courtesy of Lost in Legend*

10

CAROLINA CRYPTIDS
South Carolina's Rampaging Reptiles

South Carolina's swamps, lakes, and rivers are home to some very large reptiles. These very large and toothy beasties are commonly known as the American Alligator. Their ancestors showed up on the planet some sixty-six million years ago, and although their size has dwindled down a bit, their attitude has not. The current record for this country is 19.2 ft. and over 2,000 lbs. There are bigger ones out there.

When I dive in search of artifacts and fossils these are the creatures I share the waterways with.

Darkwater diving is diving in low visibility conditions. Blackwater diving is diving in zero visibility. This is what river diving is in South Carolina. It is not swimming along, looking at pretty fishes for hundreds of feet. It is hugging the bottom, crawling along and trying to navigate around sunken trees and logs and dodging boats when you resurface. Sounds like fun, huh?

Diving in low visibility has its fair share of problems and bumping into an alligator is the least of them, although it does happen. In these conditions you descend along an anchor line and reach the bottom, where you remain at negative buoyancy. In other words, you do not rise off the bottom and swim along as you see divers doing in beautiful places with colorful fish. If you were to rise off the bottom, the current would catch you and carry you down river. So for this very reason you crawl across the bottom, into the current, pulling yourself along the riverbed with screwdrivers lashed to your wrists with lanyards. You repeatedly stab the screwdrivers into the bottom and pull yourself along. Once you find a gravel bed you anchor yourself with one hand and search with the other.

In South Carolina rivers great visibility is six to ten feet. A lot of the time visibility is measured in inches. Average visibility is three to five inches. My light source in this type of diving comes from helmet-mounted lights with a camera attachment. This is simply because it is impossible to hold a screwdriver, collect an artifact, examine it, and bag it for a return to the surface while holding on to your light source. It does not work, and I have sacrificed a number of dive lights attempting to do this.

Now that I have set the conditions of the type of diving I do, I will now add that nothing is more invigorating than running into an alligator underwater in their element.

In 2013, I was working a project in the Combahee River in search of Native American artifacts. This was a blackwater dive, and my partner and I descended into the depths. Once at thirty feet and on the bottom my dive partner kept bumping into me. After the third time I raised up off the bottom, and with one hand anchored in the ground I let the current spin me. I tucked my knees under me and swung my other hand out to slap the other diver, grab him, and pull him in. Fortunately I missed.

That night I chastised the other diver for running into me repeatedly. I was upset that with over forty miles of river he kept attempting to occupy the same two feet that I was in. He of course adamantly denied hitting me at all.

That night I reviewed the GoPro camera footage on my helmet mount. The camera sits above the lighting system and manages to catch images in about a foot to two foot radius. Apparently I was quite fortunate when I missed slapping the other diver, because the video revealed about four feet of the alligator's tail as he swam away. It had been an approximately six to eight foot gator that had been nuzzling me. I realized just how lucky I was. I also realized just how foolish.

I decided, against my better judgement, to participate in this project in late May. I let my curiosity and excitement overrule my common sense. You see, I am well aware that May is the tail end of alligator mating season. I also know that female alligators will lay upon the bottom and a male gator will blow bubbles under their chin as they nip at him. Other male, or bull, gators will often come in and challenge the infatuated suitor and a fight will commence.

In the depth of the river the gator saw better than I did, but he did not have the intelligence to overrule his hormones. In the darkness he saw a long, dark figure blowing bubbles. In his mind he thought he was looking at a female being courted so he bumped the bubblemaker to make him leave. In this case the bubblemaker was me. Fortunately for me it was obviously a young gator and he was startled by the helmet lights. Had it been a twenty-footer I would not be here. The moral of the story is no more diving during mating season.

The second encounter happened last year in the Cooper River, when I crawled up on a submerged log pile and encountered a gator resting in the middle. After diving you begin to recognize the feel of things and texture. Large catfish feel different than logs. Also catfish move. When you run your hand along a log that is generally smooth and then realize you are now touching a log that is rough, textured, patterned, and moving you immediately realize that you have screwed up. It is at this moment that you realize you are aborting your dive. This is exactly what I did, ascending from twenty-three feet. Unfortunately she did too. I broke the surface and began drifting back toward the boat with the current. She began following me at a distance of about twenty feet.

In a moment like this you realize that if you make it back to the boat you will need a clean wetsuit and a shot of Jack Daniels. As I drifted back I inflated myself to look as large to the gator as I could. I began yelling, and then started blowing a shrill sounding whistle that I carry for such purposes. The gator turned off and watched me for a bit before slipping back under. I returned to the boat and waited for my dive buddy, Joe Harvey, to surface. When he did he gave me a hard time about harassing the gators, but we did relocate to another site.

Gators are one thing, but apparently one stretch of swamp in South Carolina is home to another unique reptile that fits into the cryptid category (cryptids are creatures whose existence is yet to be proven; Sasquatch and Chupacabra are two such creatures). This one is called the Lizard Man of Scape Ore Swamp.

On June 29, 1988, seventeen-year-old Christopher Davis was returning home at two a.m. when he had a flat tire. As he was finishing up he heard a thumping noise and turned around to see a creature running toward him. Davis stated that the creature was about twenty-five yards away, and by the time he had gotten into the vehicle and locked the door the creature was at the car. He described it as having rough green skin, three big fingers with long black nails, and red glowing eyes. He states that the creature jumped on his roof as he sped away. He was finally able to dislodge the creature, and when he got home discovered that there were deep scratches in the car roof and his side mirror was destroyed. Davis reported the incident to his family, but not much was said about it afterward until additional events began to happen in the area.

On July 14, 1988, the Lee County sheriff's office was called to the scene of a motor vehicle vandalism. Upon their arrival in Browntown, on the outskirts of Bishopville, South Carolina, they met with Tom and Mary Waye. The deputies found that the chrome molding had been stripped from the car's fenders, the sides of the car had been scratched and dented, the antenna was bent, the hood ornament was broken, and some wiring had been ripped out of the motor. They also noted that parts of the molding had actually been chewed by an animal. There were also clumps of red hair and animal footprints all over the car. As Sheriff Liston Truesdale and the sheriff's office were investigating this incident, other reports began to come in about people in the Browntown community seeing a creature about seven feet tall with red eyes. Some folks described it as green while others said it was brown. By July 16, 1988, Chris Davis's father had heard the reports, brought his son into the sheriff's office, and reported the incident from a month prior.

In the month that followed there were even more reports of a lizard-like creature and vehicles damaged. The sightings and events seemed to take place within a three-mile radius of Browntown. A couple weeks after the Davis report the sheriff's office made plaster casts of several three-toed footprints found at a scene. The prints measured fourteen inches long. According to a spokesperson of the South Carolina Marine and Resources Division, the plaster casts did not match any known creature, nor any mutated version of any known creature. Whether this is a very elaborate hoax or indeed a cryptid remains to be seen, but since the initial onslaught of events in 1988, sightings have since been sporadic, with the latest in 2015.

Scape Ore Swamp is not the only body of water to allegedly be hiding a cryptid creature within the state. Long before the Lizardman of Bishopville there was Messie. First spotted in 1933, in Lake Murray, this elusive aquatic creature has perplexed the citizens of Irmo, South Carolina, and beyond for decades.

Lake Murray is a 50,000 acre reservoir forty-one miles long. It is 200 feet deep at its deepest point and is believed to be the home of a distant cousin of the Loch Ness Monster, Nessie. Messie, as the South Carolina native is known, is suspected to be between forty to sixty feet long with a head like a snake and a tail like an eel. This is according to Gilbert Little, who first encountered the creature in 1933.

In 1980, the *Independent News* described it as "a cross between a snake and something prehistoric." Buddy Browning, his wife, and Kord Brazell were fishing on the lake when a creature surfaced and aggressively moved toward their boat. It began to aggressively crowd them as if it wanted them to leave its territory. They complied with its wishes long enough to leave and obtain a shotgun. Upon their return with the weapon they discovered the creature had left.

According to the Irmo, South Carolina, website, in 1990, a file was opened by South Carolina's Fish, Wildlife, and Parks Department—now known as the Department of Natural Resources—to track such sightings, and sightings have trickled in yearly since the original sighting.

Many folks believe that this creature could be a leftover Plesiosaur or other such creature believed to have died out around 66 million years ago. Included in those ranks is Lee Ehrlich, owner and CEO of Ghost Pros and Paranormal Divers out of Cape Coral, Florida. Lee has been researching and tracking sightings of aquatic cryptids around the country for decades, including Altie the sea monster of the Altamaha River in Georgia and the Bay Serpent off Alcatraz Island in San Francisco Bay. These creatures were believed to have been warm-blooded and breathed air, which would explain all the surface sightings in respective areas. I met Lee many years ago and worked with him on projects both in South Carolina and Florida. He believes that due to the depths of these waters these species and others may still exist. Coelacanth fish were believed to be extinct, but were rediscovered in 1938. The Omura Whale was only identified through fossils, but was rediscovered in Madagascar in 2013. These are known species once thought to be extinct. But what about new species yet identified? In 2013, a new species of shark, the Carolina Hammerhead, was discovered in South Carolina waters. As Lee puts it, our waters are the greatest unexplored territories on the planet.

Alligators in one form or another have been around for about 66 million years. They are literally living dinosaurs. But are there other prehistoric creatures still lurking in South Carolina's waterways waiting to be discovered? Are these creatures long thought to be extinct, or are they creatures yet to be discovered? Let's just hope that the next log jam I encounter in a darkwater dive is not a hungry fifty-foot Plesiosaur or a Lizardman testing his aquatic skills.

The author and Lee Ehrlich of Ghost Pros/ Paranormal Divers on site in their surveillance van. Information taken from joint investigation with various investigators was used to create the paranormal claims study.

11

A PARANORMAL CLAIMS STUDY

Lunar Influence or Lunacy?

In 2012, I wrote *Ghosts of the USS* Yorktown – *The Phantoms of Patriots Point*. I became fascinated with the ship and the many tales related to me by witnesses as I worked on that project. After its completion, I began hosting all the paranormal investigations at Patriots Point. To say that this opportunity was enlightening is a vast understatement.

On a very cold January night in 2013, I was hosting a paranormal investigation for a mother, her ghost hunting daughter, and two of her ghost hunting daughter's best friends. We entered the ship at 11:00 p.m. with the ship at residual power, meaning the ship was ninety-eight percent dark and there was no heat.

We explored the ship for a few hours and the ladies were intrigued by the muffled voices and footsteps they were hearing. In between experiences I would tell them tales of the heroes, history, and sacrifices, along with the unexplained. It was a great time.

About 2:00 a.m. we climbed up to the hangar deck and were walking through when two of the young ladies pointed toward the drink machines and asked, "Who is that?" I turned and observed a person in a dark coat and hat passing by the machines, hurrying toward the rear of the ship. I responded that it was one of the security officers and the mom reminded me that it was neither of the two we had met earlier, because one was female and the other was an older black male. This was definitely a young white male passing the drink machines, and I responded that it was just another guard and not to worry, although I kept my eye on him.

Immediately the ladies panned around with their large camper flashlights and lit up the end of the ship, and I soon realized that this individual had no reflective lettering on the back of his coat. Without the reflective "SECURITY" identifier I was concerned we had a trespasser onboard. If he got off the hangar deck and disappeared below deck we would have to shut everything down until security or law enforcement located him. I did not want to lose sight of him or let him leave the hangar deck.

I challenged the individual and he did not respond; he continued hurrying down the hangar deck in the cold. At this point I began sprinting to close the distance, and as I closed the gap he turned left toward the open stairwell. That is when I realized he was wearing a Navy issue pea coat and a hat with some writing across the forehead. This was not something that I was expecting to see. I stopped, and he took one more step and vanished directly in front of me at a distance of twenty feet.

Immediately one of the young ladies cut loose with a tirade of profanity that would have made any sailor blush. It was reassuring to know that she had just seen what I had seen and so had all the others. Soon security was coming out on to the deck and all the ladies went over to him while I regained my composure. I was amazed, unnerved, and excited all at once. My colleagues for the evening were in a state of shock, and try as we might to recreate the event, we could find no way to duplicate what we had witnessed. After about an additional hour of impromptu group therapy we all had recovered enough to drive and headed off the ship.

Remember me saying that I was looking for that one "beyond a shadow of a doubt experience" that I could just not explain no matter how hard I tried? Yup, I found it and I was immediately hooked. I soon began to intensify my collection of data on the sightings and claims experienced there and at many other locations that I had visited with paranormal investigators. As an investigator, I began looking for patterns and soon discovered something quite interesting. I began to realize that the intensity of the sighting was in direct correlation to the moon, its phases, and its percentage of lunar illumination.

Starting with the New Moon at zero percent illumination, the lunar cycle goes into a waxing phase as it builds toward a full moon at one hundred percent illumination. On the downhill side of the full moon, the lunar cycle goes into a waning phase until it burns down to a new moon again. This takes approximately 29.5 days.

For the next twenty-four months I documented every claim of paranormal activity reported at multiple locations. Through investigation quite a few experiences could be ruled out and plausibly explained; those were eliminated. Others could not be so easily explained, and in the end Lost in Legend was left with multiple "unexplainable" incidents that ranged from voices and footsteps to shadowy figures and full-bodied apparitions. These were taken into consideration and their dates of occurrence were compared to the lunar cycle.

The collective results of all these locations were extremely interesting.

I used the new moon as a starting point. There were no incidents reported three days before or three days after a new moon. During the waxing phase, as the moon was charging toward a full moon there was an increased reporting of cell phones, cameras, and other equipment losing power and their batteries being drained. At a seventy-five percent illumination in the waxing phase, there was an incident in which a tape recorder experienced a battery drain and then caught on fire. Also during the waxing phase there was an increased reporting of people feeling ill, nauseated, dizzy, and drained of energy. Perhaps something else was needing that energy and taking it from any source available.

As the illumination of the Moon increased so did the intensity of the incidents:

7% illumination there were sounds of movement and banging sounds.
26% illumination there were reports of mumbling voices heard and sounds of doors slamming.
51% illumination voices were more distinct and clear, and mists and shadowy figures were observed.

67% illumination the shadowy figures became darker and more opaque; you could no longer see through them. They also became more human-shaped.
76% illumination the ship was quite active with all of the above phenomenon.
90% physical interaction occurs. People are bumped, pushed, or touched.
92% illumination full-bodied apparitions are seen.
96% illumination there are reports of being followed and glimpsing someone tagging along, but holding back off the tour route.
99% illumination all of the above phenomenon occur with increased frequency and intensity.

By one hundred percent illumination—an actual full Moon—all types of activity are experienced, including the following:

Rattling Sounds
Clear Voices and Footsteps
Bangs and doors slamming being heard
Music being heard and displays activating
Phantom smells arising, such as cologne, cigarette smoke, coffee, laundry detergent, and fuel
Guests report being followed
Full-bodied apparitions or "Ghosts"

Interestingly enough, at this point there are no longer any shadow figures. This phenomenon disappears at approximately 92–100% illumination.

So what does this tell us?

The paranormal research community tells us that there are two types of entities: residual hauntings and intelligent hauntings. A residual haunting is as if a ghost is caught on a loop and is repeating the same actions over and over again. This type of haunting does not interact with the viewer.

The intelligent haunting deliberately interacts with the viewer by talking directly to them, following them, or even touching them. From this study, it appears that the collective hauntings are residual in nature until approximately ninety percent illumination. At this point the hauntings become intelligent hauntings and interact with the viewer. This progresses as illumination continues up to a full Moon at one hundred percent illumination. It also continues as the Moon burns down and ends at ninety percent illumination in a waning phase.

What this study suggests is that the hauntings move from a non-interactive residual nature to an intelligent nature as the Moon's illumination increases. It also tells us that the shadowy and misty figures develop and become more solid closer to the full Moon. With sightings at 90–100% illumination, this study tells us that for approximately five days—two days prior to and two days after a full Moon—chances increase significantly for seeing and experiencing a ghost. Our experience with the apparition on the hangar deck happened during a ninety-two percent waxing phase.

So what does all this mean? Does this mean that the lunar cycle plays an important part in paranormal activity, or does it mean that the more lunar activity increases, the closer to lunacy those experiencing phenomenon become? Are ghosts and ghostly activity influenced by the lunar cycles, or are we all just a little more crazy and susceptible to imagination during the full Moon?

Hampton Plantation.
Courtesy of Lost in Legend

12

TEETH, TRAILERS, TROPICAL STORMS, AND THE GHOST OF JOHN HENRY RUTLEDGE

(a.k.a. The Day I Learned I Could Cuss Underwater)

Edgar Allan Poe wrote "The Gold-Bug" at Hampton Plantation, and he and John Henry Rutledge both had a destiny with the macabre. Poe eventually began writing about the unusual and unexplained, and Rutledge eventually became the unusual and unexplained. You see, on a stormy night on March 30, 1830, a very lovesick and depressed John Henry Rutledge took his own life at Hampton Plantation in McClellanville, South Carolina. He stepped from this world into the very world that Poe would begin writing about. John Henry Rutledge became a ghost.

In 1830, John Henry Rutledge was heir to Hampton Plantation. He was from a very wealthy and prominent family and expected to marry well. Unfortunately, just like Alice Belin Flagg, he met someone far beneath his family's social status. He fell in love with the daughter of a pharmacist in Georgetown, South Carolina. His mother adamantly forbid the union, as did the father of his beloved. The pharmacist rightly believed that his daughter would not be accepted, and would always be looked down upon by the family, so he forbid John Henry Rutledge from seeing his daughter or ever setting foot in his business again.

Rutledge returned to Hampton Plantation, where he sat in his rocker near a window and just stared outside. His depression grew, and the teasing and mocking of his family only made matters worse.

On March 30, 1830, a party was being held in the downstairs ballroom. John Henry Rutledge stayed upstairs. After the party ended there was a torrential downpour that set in, and it only added to the depression that Rutledge was feeling. That evening he took a firearm, placed it against his head, and fired. After receiving the wound he still lived for an additional two days before dying. He was buried not too

The overgrown grave of John Henry Rutledge. *Courtesy of Lost in Legend*

far from the house. It is said that he still haunts the plantation, and often times the rocker is found moved to the window and rocking of its own accord.

Perhaps it was the ghost of John Henry Rutledge that plagued the Maritime Research Division (MRD) Project that Lost in Legend assisted.

MRD was conducting an underwater assessment of the area in conjunction with a land-based field study being conducted by archaeology students with the College of Charleston. MRD had already conducted remote sensing in the waterways surrounding the plantation and had discovered some excellent dive sites using side scan sonar.

Lost in Legend was along for the dive portion, which was set to begin June 5. Much like John Henry Rutledge's storm in 1830, Tropical Storm Andrea made her approach known. We spent the morning sitting in our vehicles, waiting out the storm. Rain is no problem for a diver, but once the lightning set in the mission was scrubbed for the day. No one wants to be sitting in a boat on a river when lightning is striking.

June 6 looked promising, and a brief window of clarity made us hopeful. The pontoon was launched and then the ghost of John Henry Rutledge set upon us. At least that is what we claimed.

As the trailer was being backed down the ramp the boat ramp collapsed. Apparently dirt and sand had been washed out from underneath and the weight of the pontoon boat and the trailer caused the collapse. Now the axle of the trailer was pinned against the collapsed ramp with the pontoon attached, and we were afraid that the attached truck would soon be pulled in behind it. Fortunately we were able to release the pontoon from the winch and moved it out of the way as archaeologist Nate Fulmer, Carl Naylor, and I geared up and entered the water. Ashley Deming remained with the truck as we entered the water. Immediately we were all attacked by a swarm of horseflies. They were everywhere as we were standing in chest-deep water. They were relentless. As the flies were devouring any areas not covered in a neoprene wetsuit, I responded that horseflies are extremely intelligent creatures and that I was amazed at how quickly they were able to locate four horses' posteriors wrestling with a boat trailer.

My colleagues were not amused.

Nate, Carl, and I began attempting to lift the trailer as Ashley moved the vehicle forward. This was unsuccessful. Nate and I then submerged and attempted to lift the trailer, hoping to gain greater leverage. I instantly became tangled in a discarded cast net, and as I started cutting it away I began cursing loudly. I soon had the net removed and joined Nate as we attempted to lift the trailer. Again another failure.

Our next attempt consisted of using a vehicle jack to lift the rear of the trailer up level with the remaining ramp. As we were installing this jack under the rear of the trailer it slipped and pinned Carl's foot. Nate and I were able to lift the trailer enough to release Carl, and in the process Nate managed to chip a tooth. This was done to a background of excessive underwater profanity that I was spewing into my full face mask.

Unlike a traditional regulator, a full face mask incorporates the regulator and mask into a single unit, which is often equipped with communication gear. Mine is. Although I was not utilizing the communication gear at the time, I was able to curse loudly into the mask and Nate was a captive audience directly beside me.

Eventually Nate came upon a plan to remove the jack from the tongue of the trailer and attach it to the rear, which kept it from slipping. We then jacked up the trailer as Ashley used the truck to carefully pull the trailer back on to the ramp. Eventually we were able to use a sturdier section of ramp to remove the pontoon just as our window of opportunity closed and we scrapped the mission.

At this point we decided to head back to the plantation to check on the students. As we were heading back a tire blew out on the trailer we had just rescued, forcing another delay. We changed the tire and headed back toward the plantation.

Upon arriving at the plantation, Nate and I checked in with the students and then headed out on a little land-based reconnaissance. We located some sites of possible structures, and in the process Nate almost stepped on a water moccasin who was determined not to leave her favorite sunning spot. I have to say that I was extremely impressed with Nate's dance moves and was happy he had avoided a painful and potentially fatal snakebite.

Not long after the storm hit. Tropical Storm Andrea had winds that reached 65 mph and caused four fatalities in the United States, including a South Carolina surfer who had ventured out into the water during her arrival—something that we worked very hard to avoid.

Whether it was bad luck or the ghost of John Henry Rutledge, we never did get to dive those sites that summer, but I did get a few more tales to tell and learned that I could indeed cuss underwater.

Confederate artillery regiment. *Courtesy of Lost in Legend*

13

THE LOST CANNONS OF BATTERY WARREN

Battery Warren was one of those legends I had grown up hearing as a young boy. The tales of ghostly soldiers and missing cannons had always intrigued me, so when I was older, I set out on a quest to find out what I could about this Confederate fortification.

Battery Warren was a Confederate fortress built in 1862, along the Santee River. It was an earthen fortress that held a battery of cannons facing out across the Santee River. The battery was made up of several earthen mounds utilized as parapets that were built in an L shape on a blind curve in the river. Any approaching Union gunboats had to travel head-on toward the battery's cannons, making them vulnerable and unable to return fire.

The battery received its name from a local Revolutionary War hero named Samuel Warren. Warren had once owned the property, but that was not the reason for the area being named after him. It has a lot more to do with his actions during the war, and even more with his actions after the war. During the Revolutionary War, Samuel Warren took up the patriotic cause and was harshly rebuked by an aunt in England. She advised him that if he joined the rebellion against the British she hoped that he would have an arm or leg shot off. Unfortunately she was soon to receive her wish.

In 1779, during the Siege of Savannah, Samuel Warren was an eighteen-year-old captain leading his troops in battle against the British lines when he was struck in the leg by an enemy's musket ball. This was more than likely a .75 caliber, one-ounce lead ball fired from a Brown Bess musket. Warren stood up and continued to lead his troops while supporting himself on his sword until another round struck him in the knee. He fell and was carried from the battlefield to a field hospital, where his leg was amputated. He continued to serve in administrative duties until the war ended and independence was achieved, yet he never forgot what his aunt had said to him.

After the war ended Samuel Warren, now a colonel, had a fine mahogany box crafted. He then placed his shattered leg bone inside the box. He had kept the bone from his severed leg throughout the entire war for one sole purpose. Samuel Warren had the severed limb shipped to his aunt in England with a card attached stating, "I'd rather be a one legged patriot than a two legged Royalist." Thus, a defiant American Revolutionary War hero provided the name for a defiant Confederate battery.

Construction began on the battery in 1862. As the battery was being constructed, the soldiers used Arthur Blake's Plantation as a base camp. The plantation was approximately seven miles upriver along the South Santee. On June 25, 1862, just six months before the completion of Battery Warren, Union gunboats commanded by George A. Prentiss traveled up the Santee River. Commander Prentiss had two steamers, one sloop, and one tug boat. Major S. D. Byrd sent for Capt. Christopher Gaillard's unit and his cannon, a 6-pounder rifled gun. The Confederate troops engaged the ships from the shoreline in a very short battle. The first shot had no effect, but the second shot tore through the stern of the last steamer as they moved away. Later that evening, the Union forces came ashore in an attempt to raid Blake's Plantation. Another battle was fought and two Union soldiers were killed and a few more injured, but there was no injuries or losses to the Confederacy.

By December 1862, Gaillard's Battery, now known as the Santee Light Artillery, were transferred to the newly completed Battery Warren. They had been with the site since construction began, but were now getting a chance to get settled in. The unit consisted of men from all backgrounds and heritage, but it did have a small number of German soldiers stationed. Two of these soldiers were Augustus Miller and C. F. Carlsen.

> ALTHOUGH THEIR SIGNIFICANCE IN HISTORY HAS VERY LITTLE TO DO WITH THEIR TIME AT BATTERY WARREN, THESE TWO MEN WOULD LEAVE THE BATTERY AND BECOME INVOLVED IN A TOP SECRET CONFEDERATE PROJECT. ON FEBRUARY 17, 1864, THESE TWO MEN WOULD ACCOMPANY THEIR NEW COMMANDER, LT. GEORGE E. DIXON, AND FIVE OTHERS IN AN ATTACK ON THE USS HOUSATONIC IN CHARLESTON HARBOR. THEY WOULD THEN PERISH WITH THE CREW AND SINK TO THE BOTTOM OF THE HARBOR, ENTOMBED IN THE CSS HUNLEY AFTER COMPLETING THE FIRST SUCCESSFUL SUBMARINE ATTACK IN HISTORY. THEY WOULD REMAIN IN THEIR IRON TOMB FOR THE NEXT 136 YEARS.

The encounter with Union ships on the Santee River and the Battle at Blake's Plantation prompted a greater push to finish Battery Warren, and in the collective minds of the Confederacy, Battery Warren was a necessary defense. Except it wasn't; Battery Warren never saw any action during the Civil War.

The battery was built, the men were stationed, and they were prepared to fight. As the month dragged on they soon became disheartened and felt abandoned. Not long after that the elements began to kill them. The wet and marshy environment along the river would soon take its toll on men and horses, and although the battery never actually saw combat, death was not an uncommon visitor. Even though the soldiers would only be there for a little less than two years, conditions soon became deplorable.

Some men took their chances at deserting rather than stay in the deplorable conditions. On September 15, 1863, Pvts. O. L. Wilder, Fred Williams, and Thomas Martin were the first to desert from the battery. Williams and Martin were captured on September 29, and Wilder was captured the following month on October 26. The deserters were brought back and immediately returned to their duties.

Fortunately for the soldiers, the Confederate States of America's President Jefferson Davis had issued a declaration of amnesty on August 1, 1863, to all deserters who reported back to their companies. If you returned all was forgiven. So in leaving, the men knew that if they were located, all they had to do was surrender and return to their posts. When given the choice to work or die, the soldiers decided that life at Battery Warren might not be as bad as they thought. This was also fortunate for the battery, as numbers began to dwindle due to sickness and death and they needed all the help they could get.

The battery was abandoned in March 1864. When the war did not come to them they went to the war, and Gaillard's unit did see action in McClellanville in March 1864. Even though the battery was abandoned, apparently not all have left. There have been numerous reports of disembodied voices, the sounds of horses and troop movements, and shadowy apparitions at the site over recent years. There have also been several instances at night when boaters have reported lights flickering along the battery and voices and shouting heard coming from the encampment. Another visitor reported a person wearing a Civil War kepi style cap walking through the wood line and disappearing as he approached.

According to legend, when the Santee Light Artillery left Battery Warren in March 1864, they were in a hurry to meet the Union Army in McClellanville. Several of the cannons were supposedly left behind. They remained there for quite some time, but eventually disappeared from the fortress. It is said these guns were taken as scrap and melted down not long after America entered World War II in 1941.

Another legend states that one of the first batches of cannons were brought up the Santee River by the Confederacy, but before they could reach Battery Warren a storm blew in. The Confederate barge took refuge in Chicken Creek, but the storm was greater than they anticipated and the barge overturned, sending the cannons to the bottom of the river. Two of the cannons were large Napoleon guns.

So are there cannons at the bottom of the Santee River?

Historian and archaeologist Robert G. Pasquill Jr. researched the cannons and published his findings in 1987. His breakdown follows:

From July 1862 to October 30, 1863, Battery Warren was supposed to be equipped with the following:

Two 32 Pounder (Smoothbore)
Two 12 Pounder Napoleon (Smoothbore)
Two 6 Pounder (Smoothbore)
One 6 Pounder (Rifled)
Two 3 Inch Guns (Rifled)

From October 30, 1863, to November 25, 1864, this was the inventory of the armament at Battery Warren:

Two 32 Pounder (Smoothbore)
Three 6 Pounder (Smoothbore)
One 6 Pounder (Rifled)
Four 3 Inch Guns (Rifled)

The two 12 pounder Napoleon cannons are only on the first shipment and never show up on any of the following inventories. These two cannons match the two cannons in the legend of those lost in Chicken Creek during a storm.

Could the barge containing these large cannons have been swamped in a storm? Was there a storm that could have done so? The answer to both of these questions is yes. If the guns were shipped in June to arrive at the July date, then perhaps the barge encountered a tropical storm that struck Georgia and South Carolina on June 15, 1862. This storm had winds of up to sixty miles per hour.

What is more likely is that July was the date the guns were sent to Battery Warren and not their date of arrival. If this is the case, the barge could have encountered a category two hurricane that struck Florida on August 18, with peak winds of 105 miles per hour. The winds would have diminished in intensity by the time they reached South Carolina, but the Low Country still would have received tropical storm conditions.

By December 1864 until a month after abandoning Battery Warren (April 1865), this is the armament:

Two 6 Pounders (Probably one smoothbore and one rifled)
Two 3 Inch Guns (Rifled)

Perhaps there are two large Napoleon cannons at the bottom of Chicken Creek. It is very unlikely that the Confederacy left anything behind for the Union Army to recover. No documentation has ever been located confirming the cannons were melted down during WWII. More than likely the Confederacy disabled and disposed of the cannons rather quickly, and the quickest method would be by depositing them in the river, so chances are good that the final four remaining cannons never actually left that battery and are in the river directly in front of it.

In 2015, a colleague, Roddy O'Connor, and I began to research the legends. We surveyed the battery itself and then began doing remote sensing along the river in front of the battery. Using side scan sonar and magnetometer equipment we located several anomalies of interest. We attempted to use a sub-bottom profiler, but currents were entirely too swift and almost resulted in the loss of Roddy and the $30,000 profiler.

It is our belief that the cannons are there, but torrential rains, flooding, and swift currents have prevented divers from entering the water to prove our theory.

Our results on this endeavor were reported to the Maritime Research Division, and perhaps conditions will soon allow verification that the cannons have been there all along.

Once they are located, the restless spirits of the men that attended them and died waiting on a war that never came to them can finally rest.

The Confederate soldier's diary. *Courtesy of Lost in Legend*

14

LIE OR LEGEND?
A Promise between Enemies

Although this final story has little to do with ghosts and the paranormal, I wanted to include it as an example of the research that Lost in Legend does outside the paranormal.

In February 2015, I met with the owner of a particularly interesting diary. An on-line news site called the *Charleston Mercury* had run an article on the diary which had attracted my attention and the author of the article, Robert Salvo, was gracious enough to put me in contact with the current owner, William Lind. The diary was written by a Confederate soldier and obtained by one of Mr. Lind's ancestors at the Battle of Town Creek in North Carolina. Both Bill Lind and Rob Salvo hoped to gather interest in the badly damaged diary in an attempt to help identify its author, since the book was completely devoid of his name.

The fact that an article concerning a Confederate soldier's diary was published in a news site named after the Charleston newspaper that was the first to declare that South Carolina had seceded from the Union was not lost on me.

The original *Charleston Mercury* had run an extra edition in December 1860, proudly announcing the decision and announcing the birth of the Confederacy. Now, a little over a century and a half later, this *Charleston Mercury* was asking for assistance in identifying one of the soldiers who fought in the war that followed that announcement. I was glad to offer my help.

The diary had been in Mr. Lind's family for quite some time. The legend that had been passed down through the family was that his ancestor, Sgt. Alfred G. Sturgis, had been a Union soldier during the Civil War and obtained the diary during the Wilmington Campaign in February 1865. Sturgis was a member of the 177th

Ohio Infantry; his unit was coming up the south side of the Cape Fear River after the fall of Fort Fisher and there was an engagement at Town Creek.

Sturgis stated that a Confederate soldier was lying mortally wounded and he found him. The dying soldier asked him to return the diary home to his family in Charleston. Sturgis stated that the pages that are missing were torn out because they were bloody. Also at this time his unit captured the enemy unit's flag. Sturgis has a piece of the flag on which he wrote, "The Officers took it and sent it up to headquarters and all I got was this piece. I was 18." He also recovered Confederacy currency and stationary. He wrote a letter home on this stationary.

Although the diary had been studied for over a century, the author's name is nowhere to be found in it. Markings indicate that the diary was from a member of the 27th SC Volunteer Infantry. The diary begins July 1, 1864, and the last entry was made February 19, 1865.

The known facts are that the diary was recovered during the Wilmington Campaign at the Battle of Town Creek, which took place February 18–20, 1865. The last entry was the day preceding the final date of the battle, which was February 19, 1865. Both the 27th SC Volunteer Infantry and the 177th Ohio Infantry participated in this campaign and this battle.

Mr. Lind had appointed a guardian for the manuscript and I received the diary from Col. Greg Kitchens, USMC Reserve.

After receiving the diary I took the book to a re-enactment of the Battle of Broxton Bridge. I knew that a group of re-enactors representing the 27 SC Volunteers were there and I hoped to gain some information from them.

As I was walking toward the area where the re-enactment was to take place I passed a historic recreation of the camps where the re-enactors were stationed. As I turned into the camp I saw the first flag—the flag of the 27th SC Volunteer Infantry. That was surreal in itself, but later, as I watched the re-enactment, I cannot begin to tell you how strange it is to carry a historic artifact on to a battlefield and experience the sights and sounds that the author experienced while writing the diary over a century and a half earlier.

Another surreal moment came when I spoke with the re-enactors of the 27th SC Volunteers and handed them the book. Seeing the descendants of those who had worn the same uniform they were wearing and fought beside the author of the book they were holding was surreal and uncanny.

This strange experience pushed me even harder to learn the identity of the soldier and bring the book home.

Next the diary was scanned and then analyzed page by page for relevant clues that might be important to identifying the author's responsibilities, such as his duties, associates, family and friends, background, and personal characteristics.

I was supported by author and historian Karen Stokes from the South Carolina Historical Society, author and Civil War historian Herbert O. Chambers III, and Perry J. Smith, a Civil War historian and member of the Sons of Confederate Veterans.

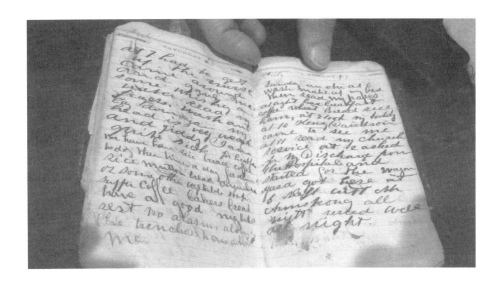

The name of the author was nowhere in the text, so clues to his identity had to be found within the pages. *Courtesy of Lost in Legend*

Re-enactors in uniform with the diary created a surreal moment.

After studying the diary this is the relevant information extracted from it:

Duties:
Reads the morning papers
Files morning reports
Files a report from the sergeants to the general
Gives out clothing
Rides in wagon frequently to wagon yard
Rides in ambulance frequently
Meets with Capt. Smith daily for dinner. The only exception is when he does so with other officers.
Damaged pages mention words such as "Drill," "Dress Parade," and "Parade"
He sleeps at night and does not have night watch or duty
Does not engage the enemy
Has access to a horse he rides into town on one occasion
Has to send up a pass for approval to go to town
Mentions Flynn of Co. H deserting. (This was later identified as James Flynn.)
Keeps tallies and purchases items
Keeps a record of incoming and outgoing personal letters

All these duties are very important to identifying rank and position.

Associates:
Contact with multiple officers, including captains, lieutenants, surgeons, and even Gen. Elliot
Rides in a wagon with Lt. McBeth and Dr. Cain
Damaged pages mention names such as "Muckenfuss" and even "Robert E. Lee"

Personal:
Writes and receives letters from Mother, Uncle, Kate, and Chip, who is also called "Dearest." She is either his wife or girlfriend
Writes letter in July to Charly Hopkins

Characteristics:
Reads "Flirtation" by Lady Charlotte Bury*
Damaged page mentions "Jane Eyre"**
Damaged page contains the word "Presbyterian"
Religious and lists scripture readings and prayers
Has evening tea with Capt. Smith*

The 27th SC Volunteer Infantry was formed by a merger of two units in September 1863: the Charleston Light Infantry Battalion and the 1st SC Battalion Sharpshooters.

The newly formed 27th SCV was then assigned to Gen. Hagood's Brigade. According to Gen. Johnson Hagood in his memoirs:

> The Twenty-Seventh was especially claimed by Charlestonians as their regiment, and in consequence of its local popularity many of the best young men of the city were in its ranks. The average intelligence and social position of the rank and file were thus greater than most regiments. It was not equal to some others in its discipline, but under Gaillard, or any of its officers who possessed its confidence, it would go anywhere and do anything. . . . There was too much intelligence and too little rigidity of discipline in its ranks for men without force of character to command it successfully. This regiment . . . had served only in South Carolina but it had been peculiarly fortunate in its service. It had won honor in the Fort at Secessionville in '62; had been Taliferro's mainstay at Wagner on the 18th. July; a portion of it had been Elliot's garrison at Sumter when the boat attack was repulsed; and two of its sharpshooter regiments had obtained honorable mention at Pocotaligo.

The Civil War Soldiers and Sailors database lists 1,960 men on the roster for this unit, and author Randolph W. Kirkland Jr., in his comprehensive study of Civil War dead *Broken Fortunes*, lists 237 dead from this unit during the Civil War.

In beginning research, Lost in Legend started at the battle to eliminate the obvious. Using *Broken Fortunes*, it was learned that only one individual from the 27th South Carolina Volunteer Infantry was killed at the Battle of Town Creek: Pvt. A. A. Grant of Co. D, who was eighteen years old. He was killed outright, affording no opportunity for interaction with Sgt. Sturgis. His rank also did not match the duties.

Pvt. Thomas C. Egan of Co. H was grievously wounded on the last day of the battle. He died from his wounds, but again, his rank did not match the duties of the author of the diary.

At this point Lost in Legend began to eliminate command staff, and as of March 8, 2015, all command staff were eliminated. Also sixteen officers, the only sergeant major, and two first sergeants were eliminated. All medical staff were also eliminated. From here Lost in Legend began to look at the rank of adjutant.

This position was originally filled by W. M. Smith, who died from illness in June 1864. The position then went to Lt. A. A. Allemong, who was killed that month, and then to Lt. G. B. Gelling, who was also subsequently killed in June. By the end of

---

* The two books mentioned are by English authors and contain English customs. The tea issue is common in English culture, but also Irish culture. What was interesting to note and later became valuable information was that Company H of the 27th South Carolina Volunteer Infantry consisted of Irish volunteers.

the month, Lt. Alfred Drayton Simons had been appointed adjutant. That also coincided with the July 1 beginning of the diary. Simons had the background and education, along with social connections, and a few of the duties also seemed to fit. He was also captured at the Battle of Town Creek and spent the remainder of the war in a Union prison. Further research discovered that he already had a diary in the SC Historical Society. The handwritings did not match and the diaries overlapped. This eliminated Simons.

Lost in Legend then learned of two manuals written by August Kautz. Kautz was a German-American soldier and Union Army cavalry officer during the American Civil War. He was the author of several army manuals on duties and customs eventually adopted by the US military:

The Company Clerk (1863)
Customs of Service for Non-Commissioned Officers and Soldiers (1864)
Customs of Service for Officers (1866)

The manuals became invaluable.

Lost in Legend further ruled out the position of adjutant using *Customs of Service for Officers*. One interesting note was that this position was required to keep track of incoming and outgoing mail. The author of the diary had a listing of all incoming and outgoing letters listed in the back of his diary. This was the obvious purpose of that. If he was not the adjutant, then he would be able to provide a list when requested.

In *Customs of Service for Non-Commissioned Officers and Soldiers* (1864) there was a new position noted: quartermaster sergeant. All the duties mentioned in the diary fit this position:

> A REGIMENTAL quartermaster sergeant is allowed to each regiment or battalion in the army. A quartermaster sergeant is also allowed to each company in the cavalry and in the Fifth Artillery. The former belongs to the non-commissioned staff and the latter is mustered on the company rolls next below the first sergeant. They both receive the same pay and allowances,—regimental and company quartermaster sergeants,—viz.: twenty-two dollars per month, an allowance of clothing, and one ration. Just a few of the duties listed in this manual summed up the majority of what the author described in his daily entries.
>
> The quartermaster sergeant of the regiment is appointed by the regimental commander, on the recommendation of the quartermaster of the regiment, and should be exclusively under the orders of the latter . . .

The duties of this sergeant are to take the immediate charge of the property for which the regimental quartermaster is responsible, and direct the employees and the details sent to work for the quartermaster department.

In the evening, between retreat and tattoo, the sergeant should report to the quartermaster how he has succeeded in the performance of the duties of the day, and receive his instructions for the morrow.

Lost in Legend now believed that the author of the diary was the quartermaster sergeant of the 27th SC Volunteers, but unfortunately none of the sources detailing the 27th South Carolina Volunteer Infantry listed any quartermaster sergeants.

We returned to the diary and learned that Capt. Robert Press Smith was the quartermaster and the author of the diary reported to him at dinner. Tattoo and Retreat are bugle calls, and dinner would fall in between those, also lending credibility to the belief that the author was a quartermaster sergeant based on Kautz's manual.

This was the break we were looking for.

Capt. R. P. Smith was also quartermaster with the 1st SC Sharpshooters, one of the units that originally merged to become the 27th SC Volunteers. In cross referencing the 27th SCV with the 1st SC Sharpshooters, it was learned that Capt. Smith collaterally transferred in that position. Perhaps his quartermaster sergeant did also, as the 1st SC had two listed:

E. W. Macbeth

A. J. MacCaughrin

Out of the two, it was eventually discovered that A. J. McCaughren was also transferred to the 27th SC Volunteers as a quartermaster sergeant.

Andrew Jackson McCaughrin was born October 4, 1838, and died November 19, 1895, meaning he survived the war. Research also showed that he was not captured; he was at Town Creek and apparently escaped.

His service in the Confederacy began in 1861, when he enlisted in the Calhoun Guard. On April 20, 1863, he was promoted to sergeant. He served with the 1st SC Sharpshooters and then merged into the 27th SC Volunteers. He was Irish, which would explain the interest in literature choices and the evening tea. It would also explain his interest in James Flynn from the Irish Volunteers deserting . . . the only mention of any soldier deserting.

He was from Newberry, South Carolina, but he and his brothers moved to Charleston with their Uncle Samuel McCaughrin, who was a book keeper. They fled the Yellow Fever epidemic of 1854 and returned to Newberry. A. J. McCaughrin worked as a book keeper for P. J. Caldwell, and also for Kennedy and Crawford. (There was a partnership in a general store with Mcaughren and Carwile in Newberry.) After the war he became a director for Etiwan Phosphate Company in Charleston.

His father died in 1863, and was deceased at the time of the diary. The uncle he wrote to was Samuel McCaughrin. His mother had died in 1854, when he was sixteen. His aunt, uncle, and parents are all listed in the same household in the 1860 census. It is believed when he refers to mother in his diary he is speaking of his aunt.

He writes to Charley Hopkins in July. Lt. Charles Mitchell Hopkins was a lieutenant in the 27th SC Volunteers. His brother was also a captain in the 27th SCV. Capt. James Ward Hopkins was killed in June. It is believed that Lt. Hopkins was on furlough, taking care of his brother's affairs in Charleston, when McCaughrin wrote to him. Not identifying him by rank shows a personal relationship outside a military one. The Hopkins brothers also had a sister named Katherine L. Hopkins, or "Kate." She was approximately two years older than McCaughrin, and it is believed she is the Kate he was writing to.

"Dearest Chip" remains unidentified.

A. J. McCaughrin is buried in Rosemont Cemetery (Section B4) in Newberry, South Carolina.

In searching records, Lost in Legend obtained copies of his muster records after a trip to Columbia, South Carolina, and a day of research in the SC History and Archives. A handwritten document was obtained on-line and was compared to that of the diary.

Although this retired criminal investigator has limited experience in document comparison, the standard was to have a minimum of six points of identification and comparative matches. Between the two documents I made thirteen. This was enough to forward it to another colleague with more experience in documents and handwriting analysis who concluded that based off the comparison of the known document written by Quartermaster Sergeant Andrew Jackson McCaughrin to the unknown author's writing in the diary McCaughrin was the author of both.

So if the diary belonged to Sgt. McCaughrin and he survived the Battle at Town Creek, then how did Sgt. Sturgis obtain the diary?

In reviewing Sgt. Sturgis's letters to his mother, we begin with a young man who is eager to travel and fight for his country. He writes about seeing cotton for the first time and watching as it is picked. As the letters continue, he writes that his close friend and tent mate, Latham Coleman, was left behind in the hospital as the regiment moved on to Murfreesboro. Coleman had been ill and his health continued to deteriorate. Sturgis holds on to his friend's pocketbook and watch, only to later learn his friend has died, and that he will now have to hold on to his friend's possessions until he can return them to the young man's mother. The letters also show a change in the young man.

Likewise, Sgt. McCaughrin also became sick on July 2, 1864. By July 13, he had dysentery, and two days later was hospitalized. By July 17, he was discharged and far more fortunate than Latham Coleman.

On the morning of February 20, 1865, as exhausted Union troops were marching along the Federal Point Road they stopped for a brief rest. A young corporal requested permission from his commanding officer to visit a house on the side of the road. The young man advised that it was his childhood home and he had been raised there, and desired to see his mother. Upon stopping at the residence he was greeted by his ecstatic mother, who informed him of how fortunate she was to have seen both her sons in two days. She advised his brother had stopped by the day before as Confederate forces had marched by. The Union soldier was Cpl. Jacob Horne of the 2nd North Carolina US Infantry, who was most likely assigned as a scout to the Union forces. This would have been done due to his familiarity with the area. His brother was Confederate soldier Cpl. Hosea Horne, in Capt. Thomas Southerland's Wilmington Horse Artillery, 1st North Carolina Artillery. The overjoyed mother was so excited and relieved to see her two sons that she did not realize they were both marching toward a confrontation that would bring them together face-to-face in combat.

The Wilmington Campaign was an effort by Union forces to take Wilmington from the Confederacy. Wilmington was the last major Confederate port on the Atlantic seacoast, and Fort Fisher on the Cape Fear River protected it. If Fort Fisher was taken then there would be little to stop the Union from seizing Wilmington and cutting off the only means of supply to the Confederacy. Capturing Wilmington would mean the beginning of the end of the Confederacy.

The first campaign against Fort Fisher in December 1864 was unsuccessful. Maj. Gen. Benjamin Butler was relieved of his command and Maj. Gen. Alfred Terry was selected to make a second attempt. When his troops landed they fought their way up the beach. The confrontation was hand-to-hand and at point blank range. The Union troops seized Fort Fisher in this second bloody attempt and drove the Confederates out. Those that fled retreated to Fort Buchanan, which also fell to Union forces.

At this point Gen. John Schofield was given the responsibility of taking Wilmington. He had 12,000 men under his command and Sgt. Alfred G. Sturgis of the 177th Ohio Infantry was one of them.

On the other side was approximately half that number of men. They were exhausted and scattered. By now they had learned of the fall of Fort Fisher.

Much like our Union counterpart, our author, Sgt. McCaughrin, has also become tired and weary of war. His last entry in the diary shows as much:

Sunday
The enemy erected a battery on the left of
They were a part of Thomas's army Schoffield's Corp at 10 it was found

They having an inferior force has extended their lines threatening our line of retreat
Evacuated bringing all off to safety. The enemy did not follow.
Retreated about 60 miles to town,
I have just heard that Charleston was-
Evacuated on the 17th
Oh how I hardly care what becomes of the country
None of the pickets from our company were captured
Read a church service
-- Wilmington Beach. The enemy followed.

By Sunday, February 19, Confederate forces were exhausted as they took up a defensive position at Town Creek. They had been pushed and scattered by advancing Union forces that doubled their size. The Union forces had become more and more aggressive with each victory as they moved toward Wilmington. Sgt. McCaughrin has obviously received the news that on February 18, 1865, Charleston fell to Union forces. At this point, tired and exhausted, he and many others are now awaiting their fate.

When the fighting at Town Creek began it was also hand-to-hand, as were most of the Wilmington conflicts. A Confederate soldier of the 11th South Carolina Infantry was shot at such close range that the Union soldier was able to see the cartridge paper protruding from the soldier's facial wound as he fell dead to the ground.

Exhausted, the Confederate troops made a stand and held their ground as best they could. Bravery was not uncommon on both sides this date. One cannon, "St. Paul," was a 12 pounder howitzer belonging to the Edenton Bell Battery. Four bells from area churches had been donated to the Confederate cause and used in the making of the four cannons of the unit. St. Paul was named in honor of St. Paul's Episcopal Church in Edenton that donated its bell used in that cannon's construction.

A Union soldier fought his way up to the Confederate line and demanded the surrender of the gun and its crew as it was preparing to fire. "If you fire that gun I will kill you," he shouted. "Kill and be damned," was the response he received from Sgt. Benjamin F. Hunter as he ordered his artilleryman to fire. The cannon erupted and case shot filled the air as it struck Company H of the 104th Ohio Infantry at point blank range, killing and wounding over twenty of them. Union troops immediately killed the gunner and were preparing to kill Sgt. Hunter had their lieutenant not intervened and spared him by stating, "He's too brave a man to be killed."

The Confederate forces stood as long as they could. Many surrendered. Others fled, but were captured and spent the remainder of the war in federal prison camps. Some were fortunate and escaped, and it appears that Sgt. A. J. McCaughrin was one of the fortunate.

On February 20, 1865, Oliver Hughes of the 12th Kentucky Infantry captured the battle flag of the 11th SC Infantry. It was an action for which he would later earn the Congressional Medal of Honor.

In a letter written on Confederate stationary and dated February 22, 1865, Sgt. Sturgis states, "I found this paper and envelope in ones knapsack. They threw most everything away in their haste. I found a part of their flag they tore up to keep us from getting it."

The 27th SC Volunteers were staunch protectors of their flag and would have definitely destroyed it before seeing it captured. Their valiant history of defending this flag started November 28, 1863, when Confederate forces had already captured Ft. Sumter and were themselves now defending it from a Union attack.

Pvt. James Tupper Jr. saw their unit flag shot down on Fort Sumter. He walked the entire length of the wall on the parapet while under fire to raise it. When he got to the flag he found the staff damaged and too short. He improvised, creating a splice staff, and he and his comrades raised the flag under heavy fire. One shot actually ripped it from their hands, yet they once again retrieved it and raised it.

It appears that there was no valiant exchange between Sgt. Alfred G. Sturgis and a dying Confederate soldier after all. The letter that Sturgis wrote appears to answer the question as to how he acquired the diary: he found it. The Wilmington Campaign was successful, and on May 9, 1865, the war officially ended. Perhaps after the war Sturgis concocted the entire tale of receiving the diary from a dying Confederate soldier for a better "war story" to tell his grandchildren. Maybe the tale was more lie than legend.

Not so fast. Remember earlier I mentioned a member of the 27th SC Volunteers named Pvt. Thomas C. Egan? He was wounded in the battle of Town Creek and later died in a hospital from his wounds.

Tommy Egan was an Irishman assigned to Company H. This is the same company to which the deserter James Flynn belonged.

Tommy Egan was grievously injured. He died in an enemy hospital at Town Creek. The hospital that he died in was part of the 177th Ohio Infantry, the same unit Sgt. Sturgis served in.

Is it possible that Egan was carrying McCaughrin's diary and Sturgis did indeed come into contact with the dying Egan, or did Sturgis simply recover the diary from a discarded knapsack? The answer to that we will never know.

Regardless, Lost in Legend researched the author's descendants, thus notifying them of the diary. In 2016, the diary was returned to Charleston and the promise, whether real or fabricated, was fulfilled 151 years later.

The author . . . now. *Courtesy of Jon Jackson Photography*

CONCLUSION
Final Thoughts

Behind every legend there is an element of truth. There is always history behind a haunting and facts within folklore. One just has to take the time and dig a little deeper.

If there is such a thing as a ghost, perhaps we owe it to them to do this. Perhaps in doing so we are able to tell the tales that they lived and died creating with an element of historic accuracy.

It is my hope that books such as this will never let our legends get lost.

It is also my mission to never let the facts get Lost in Legend.

BIBLIOGRAPHY

Butler, Lindley S. *Pirates, Privateers, & Rebel Raiders of the Carolina Coast*. Chapel Hill: UNC Press, 2000.

Butler, Nicholas Michael. *Votaries of Apollo: The St. Cecilia Society and the Patronage of Concert Music in Charleston, South Carolina, 1766–1820*. Columbia: University of South Carolina Press, 2007.

Buxton, Geordie, and Ed Macy. *Haunted Harbor: Charleston's Maritime Ghosts and the Unexplained*. Charleston: History Press, 2005.

"The Salem Witch Trials and South Carolina?" *Carolina Traveler*, October 27, 2015.

Cordingly, David. *Under the Black Flag: The Romance and Reality of Life among the Pirates*. New York: Random House, 1996.

Dean, Carolina. "Mary Ingelman: The First Witch of Winnsboro, South Carolina."

Dobson, Mary. *Disease: The Extraordinary Stories behind History's Deadliest Killers*. London: Quercus Books, 2008.

Duffus, Kevin P. *The Last Days of Black Beard the Pirate*. Raleigh: Looking Glass Productions, 2008.

Fonvielle, Chris E., Jr. *The Wilmington Campaign – Last Rays of Departing Hope*. Mechanicsville: Stackpole Books, 2001.

Fraser, Walter J. Jr. *Charleston! Charleston!* Columbia: University of South Carolina Press, 1989.

Fraser, Walter J., Jr. *Lowcountry Hurricanes – Three Centuries of Storms at Sea and Ashore*. Athens: The University of Georgia Press, 2006.

Hart, Charles Henry. *Historical Descriptive and Critical Catalogue of the Works of American Artists in Collection of Herbert L. Pratt*. Pittsfield: Sun Printing, 1917.

Hart, Robert L. *Rivers, Rice, and Rebellion: The Search for a Battery*. Columbia: US Forestry Service, 1980.

Hastings, Max. *The Oxford Book of Military Anecdotes*. New York: Oxford University Press, 1985.

Hudson, Charles. *The Southeastern Indians*. Knoxville: University of Tennessee Press, 1976.

Hutchisson, James. "The Rites of St. Cecilia." *Charleston Magazine*, March 2006.

Kajencki, Annmarie Francis. *Count Casimir Pulaski: From Poland to America, a Hero's Fight for Liberty*. New York: Rosen Publishing Group, 2005.

Kent, James A. *Riegel's Handbook of Industrial Chemistry (Eighth Edition)*. Van Nostrand Reinhold, 1983.

Lyle, Katie Letcher. *The Man Who Wanted Seven Wives: The Greenbrier Ghost and the Famous Murder Mystery of 1897*. Charleston: Quarrier Press, 1999.

Martin, Margaret Rhett. *Charleston Ghosts*. Columbia: University of South Carolina Press, 1963.

McTeer, J. E. *Fifty Years as a Low Country Witch Doctor*. Beaufort: Beaufort Book Company, 1976

McTeer, J. E. *High Sheriff of the Low Country*. Beaufort, South Carolina: Beaufort Book Company, 1970.

Michelsohn, Lynn. *Lowcountry Hurricanes*. Roswell: Cleanan Press, Inc., 200.

Miller, Page Putnam. *Fripp Island: A History*. Charleston: History Press, 2006.

Moore, Francis M. *Ghosts or Devils, I'm Done: The Startling Adventure of Two Officers of the 62nd Ohio Infantry on Polly Island, SC during General Gilmore's siege of Fort Sumpter in the War of the Rebellion and the Story Which Incited Their Adventure*. Deadwood: O. C. Cole and Sons, 1908.

Orr, Bruce. *Ghosts of Berkeley County, South Carolina*. Charleston: History Press, 2011.

Pasquill, Robert G., Jr. *Battery Warren and The Santee Light Artillery*. Columbia: Berkeley County Historical Society, 1987.

Peterkin, Genevieve C. *Heaven Is a Beautiful Place: A Memoir of The South Carolina Coast*. Columbia: University of South Carolina Press, 2000.

Receipt Book of Carolina Dean . . . and Blessed Teachings. Blog. 2013.

Rhyne, Nancy. *Tales of the South Carolina Low Country*. Winston-Salem: John F. Blair Publishing Company, 1982.

Roberts, Nancy. *Ghosts of the Carolinas*. Columbia: University of South Carolina Press, 1962.

Roberts, Nancy. *South Carolina Ghosts from the Coast to the Mountains*. Columbia: University of South Carolina Press, 1983.

Stringer-Robinson, Gretchen. *Folly Beach: A Brief History*. Charleston: History Press, 2006.

Willcox, Clarke A. *Musings of a Hermit at Three Score and Ten*. Charleston: Walker, Evans, and Cogswell Company, 1973.

From *Wilson, David K. The Southern Strategy: Britain's Conquest of South Carolina and Georgia, 1775–1780*. Columbia: University of South Carolina Press, 2005.

Zepke, Terrance. *Ghosts of the Carolina Coasts, Haunted Lighthouses, Plantations, and other Historic Sites*. Sarasota: Pineapple Press, 1999.

Zepke, Terrence. *Pirates of the Carolinas*. Sarasota: Pineapple Press, 2005.

ACKNOWLEDGMENTS

I would like to thank the following people and organizations:

The Maritime Research Division of South Carolina:
    Nate Fulmer – Archaeologist
    Ashley Deming – Archaeologist
    Carl Naylor
    Joe Beatty
    Jim Spirek
The South Carolina Institute for Archaeology and Anthropology
The South Carolina Historical Society
The South Carolina Department of Archives and History
The Charleston Library Society
The Charleston County Library
The Berkeley County Library
The Dorchester County Library
All Saints Church
Belin United Methodist Church:
    Katherine Durning – Historian
Swamp Fox Diving and Rick Presnell
Charlie Fox
Spirit Hunters:
    Pamela Nance and Ashley Field
Ghost Pros/Paranormal Divers and Lee Ehrlich
Charleston Scuba and Tom and Sally Robinson
Fort Sumter Tours
Bulldog Tours and John LaVerne
Yorktown Ghost Tours and Craig Delk
Charleston Pirate Tours and Eric Lavender and Sabrina Lavender
Roddy O'Connor
Joe Harvey
Central True Value Hardware
Tom Rabon
Jon Jackson
William "Bill" Lind

Col. Greg Kitchens, USMC Reserves
The 27th SC Infantry reenactment unit
Sons of Confederate Veterans
Perry and Danielle Smith
The North Carolina Department of Natural and Cultural Resources
The Mead Art Museum
Karen Stokes
Herbert O. Chambers III

ABOUT THE AUTHOR

After retiring from law enforcement, Bruce Orr combined his love for history and legends with his love for investigations and writing and developed a research and consulting company known as Lost in Legend. He has spent the past several years researching the history behind the legends and folklore he grew up hearing about and documenting those tales, and the history behind them, for future generations to enjoy. *Lost in Legend* is his fifth book covering stories from his home state of South Carolina.